MW00638805

Group's **EMERGENCY RESPONSE**

handbook

for: **WOMEN'S MINISTRY**

Group

Loveland, Colorado

www.group.com

Group resources actually work!

This Group resource helps you focus on **"The 1 Thing"®**—a life-changing relationship with Jesus Christ. "The 1 Thing" incorporates our **R.E.A.L.** approach to ministry. It reinforces a growing friendship with Jesus, encourages long-term learning, and results in life transformation, because it's:

Relational
Learner-to-learner interaction enhances learning and builds Christian friendships.

Experiential
What learners experience through discussion and action sticks with them up to 9 times longer than when they simply hear or read.

Applicable
The aim of Christian education is to equip learners to be both hearers and doers of God's Word.

Learner-based
Learners understand and retain more when the learning process takes into consideration how they learn best.

Group's Emergency Response Handbook for Women's Ministry

Copyright © 2008 Group Publishing, Inc.

Visit our Web site: **www.group.com**

Credits
Contributors: Linda Crawford; Heather Dunn; Kelly Schimmel Flanagan, Ph.D.; Paul Friesen, Ph.D.; Laura Greiner, Ph.D.; Rebekah Knight-Baughman, Ph.D.; Joy-Elizabeth F. Lawrence; Renee Madison, LPC; Maggie H. Robbins, M.A.; Christina Schofield; Amber Van Schooneveld; Terri S. Watson, Psy.D.; and Amy Weaver
Chief Creative Officer: Joani Schultz
Editor: Janna Kinner, MSW
Senior Developer: Amy Nappa
Project Manager: Jan Kershner
Copy Editor: Michael Van Schooneveld
Senior Designer: Andrea Filer
Book Designer/Print Production Artist: Pamela Poll Graphic Design
Cover Art Director/Designer: Jeff A. Storm
Illustrator: Pamela Poll
Production Manager: DeAnne Lear

Unless otherwise indicated, all Scripture quotations are taken from the Holy Bible, New Living Translation, copyright © 1996, 2004. Used by permission of Tyndale House Publishers, Inc., Carol Stream, IL 60188. All rights reserved.

Library of Congress Cataloging-in-Publication Data

Group's emergency response handbook for women's ministry /
[contributors, Linda Crawford ... et al.].
    p. cm.
  ISBN-13: 978-0-7644-3653-6 (pbk. : alk. paper) 1. Church work with
women. 2. Life change events. 3. Life change events–Religious
aspects–Christianity. I. Crawford, Linda, 1938- II. Title: Emergency
response handbook for women's ministry.
  BV4445.G76 2007
  259.082-dc22

                              2007036555

10 9 8 7 6 5 4 3 2 1   17 16 15 14 13 12 11 10 09 08

Printed in the United States of America.

Contents

Introduction

It's not easy going through divorce. Or dealing with depression. Or facing breast cancer. It's hard and painful and brutal.

But it doesn't have to be lonely.

Christians should never have to face trials on their own. Those around them—their Christian brothers and sisters—should rise up and support them.

"Share each other's burdens, and in this way obey the law of Christ" (Galatians 6:2).

Although it isn't easy going through trials, it's also tough being on the outside and trying to help those who are suffering. You don't know what to do. You're worried about hurting their feelings or stepping on their toes or saying the exact *wrong* thing. Of course you care—you love them! It isn't that you don't want to help—it's just that you don't know how.

Group's Emergency Response Handbook for Women's Ministry will help you come alongside those in your ministry who are facing tough times. From care and counseling tips to practical ideas for what to say and what not to say, this book offers insight after insight into how to care for the hurting.

Naturally, it would be great if you never had to pick up this book! But the reality is that everyone faces tough times—including the women in your church. And they need your help.

So when a woman you love is going through infertility, dealing with an eating disorder, or has just been diagnosed with breast cancer…it's time to pick up this guide. Use the table of contents to find the specific hurt for which you're caring, and then flip to that section.

Once there, you'll find a **real-life narrative**—a story from someone who's been there. Sometimes it's inspiring, and you'll read how support and love sustained someone through a hard time. Other times it's disappointing and tells of people left alone during tragedy or rejected during trial. Either way, the story will move you, and show you the importance of devoted friends.

Each section also includes **care and counseling tips** that will give you practical ideas for reaching out in love. From baking dinner, to helping with rides to appointments, to intentional listening, these ideas will help you effectively support the hurting people in your women's ministry.

Next, you'll find **group tips**, so you can include other women in your ministry in reaching out to your hurting friend. These practical ideas will help support and love the woman through her pain.

And, finally, you'll find an invaluable section on **what to say and what not to say** to your friend. The words we use can help or hurt a friend more than we know. This section will help you avoid the hurtful comments and use the helpful ones.

You'll also find useful boxes in each section that offer Scripture help, guidelines for referring your friend to a professional counselor, and additional resources, such as books and Web sites, that you can use as you support your hurting friend.

Our prayer for this book is that it will help you help a friend during a difficult time.

> "He comforts us in all our troubles so that we can comfort others. When they are troubled, we will be able to give them the same comfort God has given us" (2 Corinthians 1:4).

The names and identifying information of the women who have shared their stories have been changed.

The information in this book is meant to be a guide for you to handle emergencies that women and families in your ministry face. It is not meant to replace advice you receive from licensed counselors or psychologists, and should not be considered legal advice.

CHAPTER ONE

Breast Cancer
Supporting Women on the Road to Recovery

with counseling insights from **MAGGIE H. ROBBINS, M.A.**

+ ministry tips from **HEATHER DUNN**

Sonia is the first to admit that she's great at denial. She admitted that she had breast cancer, but only to a few. She didn't really talk about it much at the time but now admits that sharing helps.

Emergency Response Handbook: *How did you feel when you first found out you had breast cancer?*

Sonia: Numb. I was totally numb. I couldn't move. I didn't even know what questions to ask. The nurses were used to this daily occurrence and they were quite patient. Fortunately, my kids were at camp, so I didn't have to face them right away. My husband was with me. He was just as stunned. What saved me was my friend Fran. I must have called her, though I don't remember. All I remember is that she said, "This is a survivor's cancer and you're not going to go through this alone. I'll be over in an hour and I'm bringing dinner." That saved my life.

ERH: *What impact did your breast cancer have on your family?*

Sonia: It turned out to be a good thing that I had a little time before my kids came home. It gave me time to think about what to tell them. Basically, I didn't want them worrying, so I kept the information to a minimum. None of us talked about it very much. Honestly, I didn't want to talk about it, so the others didn't either.

ERH: *What impact did your breast cancer have on your work?*

Sonia: I didn't really let anyone know the magnitude of my inner feelings. People knew that I had breast cancer, but I didn't really let them know what all was going on. I was gone a week for my surgery and then was back—I just wanted to get everything over with as soon as possible. I work for a Christian organization and I didn't even put it on the prayer chain or weekly updates with my co-workers. Since I work primarily with men, I tried to be mostly factual and get to work. So I stuffed my feelings and went about things as usual.

ERH: *What treatment did you have?*

Sonia: I had one breast completely removed right away. After the surgery, the doctors said they thought they had gotten it all, so I didn't do chemo or radiation or anything else. Everything was over in a week. I know some women have lots more to deal with than I did.

ERH: *What impact did your breast cancer have on your health?*

Sonia: I do self-exams and have a check up with my doctor every six months. There's always this cloud that the cancer could come back at any time. There's never a guarantee that it's gone, so I'm pretty careful to keep my appointments.

I also have new priorities. God gives us opportunities to grow through trials. I took up running and now run marathons. I started with a 39-mile walk for breast cancer research. Now I run several mornings a week. I follow a regimen that prevents injury and is good for my body. I love it and wouldn't trade it for anything.

ERH: *What's the greatest lesson you've learned from breast cancer?*

Sonia: There's support and compassion—you just have to reach for it. My friends, those that I told, were extremely supportive. My husband was wonderful, too.

ERH: *What impact did your breast cancer have on your relationship with your husband?*

Sonia: He was wonderful throughout the process, very supportive. I have found that it's harder for me to be intimate. Missing one breast makes you feel very different in this regard. I opted not to have reconstructive surgery—it didn't feel right for me. Fortunately, my relationship with my husband is Christ-focused and has never been based on our sexual pleasures. If it had been, we'd both be having lots more trouble. I've been working on learning how to love again, in a different way. It's a tough thing to work through.

ERH: *What's the most helpful thing someone did for you?*

Sonia: There were two, actually. I already mentioned my friend who told me I would survive and brought dinner the first night. The other was a friend who took me to lunch within a couple of days. She gave me some great resources with lots of information about breast cancer. That was really helpful.

ERH: *What was the most difficult thing someone said or did?*

Sonia: Some comments, though they were well-intentioned, felt harsh at the time. One comment I remember was, "If I had breast cancer, my husband would divorce me!" Where I didn't have doubts about my husband's support before, now I wondered what I'd done to him and how he was really feeling. I remember I called him right after the conversation just to hear that extra reassurance that all was OK.

ERH: *Where was God?*

Sonia: This was surprising to me. My experience wasn't a huge spiritual high. My big question for God was, "Do you really care?" I told God, "Now I'm really going to put you to the test." I wondered if God was too big and too busy to care about me personally. It was a real test of my faith. I realized that I was trying to define God in human terms, make him too human. Looking back, I can see how much God did care.

I had to evaluate how I define myself, too, and God helped me do that. Breast cancer takes away your dignity and your sex appeal is under attack. You wonder if you're attractive and worth loving. God gives the unconditional "yes." I wonder how people go through this experience without God. It's hard enough with him!

ERH: *What would you do differently if you could?*

Sonia: I'd talk more with my family and friends. I'd get more help. I'm surprised as I look back at how much I stuffed it. Looking back, I get pretty emotional. I'm not sure I'd tell my kids much more, and I still wouldn't wear my emotions on my sleeve for all to see, but I would share more with my husband and friends. There are great Web sites now for women with breast cancer. You can share what you're going through and talk with others: www.mylifeline.org and www.caringbridge.com are two that I'm aware of.

I'd keep better track of things, too. A friend wisely advised me to get a notebook and keep a journal of dates, medicines, and treatments. I didn't do that as thoroughly as I should have, and now I wish I had. It would help me when I need to remember what happened when I go to current doctor's appointments. I can't believe how hard it is to remember things that I thought I would never forget. I could use the notebook now to help others, too.

ERH: *How do you feel when you hear someone talking about breast cancer today?*

Sonia: Guilty. I know others who had a much more difficult time and I feel guilty that mine went so well. My heart goes out to them, too, because I know what they're going through. I also worry that they may have a harder time.

ERH: *Is there any advice you'd give to someone facing breast cancer?*

Sonia: Take a friend to all your appointments. My husband came to some of the appointments, but he was as numb as I was. Take someone who's less emotionally attached. There's no way you can remember everything your doctor says, and when you're numb you really can't remember much of anything. Your friend can take notes, remember the questions you had on your way over in the car, and help you debrief later.

Care and Counseling Tips

THE BASICS

A breast cancer diagnosis is devastating and life-altering. Treatment has come a long way making survival more likely—however, for many a patient, a cancer diagnosis seems like a death sentence. The shocking news can affect mind, body, and spirit.

✛ Mind

How one reacts to the news after the initial shock has worn off can determine her relationship to their illness and the likelihood of survival. Many women are determined to fight and take an active role in their treatment and recovery. Others succumb to their cancer and end up feeling overwhelmed by their lack of power in the situation.

✛ Body

Women with breast cancer lose their health and energy. They often struggle with a negative body image. They can lose their breasts, which can affect their sexual identity. Hair loss is a common side effect from treatment and can cause embarrassment and draw attention to her battle with cancer. Eventually, she may lose her life as her body betrays her.

✛ Spirit

For most women, the initial reaction is denial or disbelief. Grief is an inevitable emotion, as there is loss after loss during their fight with cancer. Any illness causes a role shift, as the woman has to learn to be taken care of instead of being the caretaker. She may lose her career and her social network. Ultimately, she may lose her life and any plans for the future vanish. Losses compound to make living with cancer one of the most difficult challenges in a woman's life. A spiritual crisis is likely, as she has to face the meaning of life and death.

Care Tips

When you learn that a woman in your ministry has been diagnosed with breast cancer, there are several ways to help her as she adjusts and moves forward.

+ Help with day-to-day chores.
The initial shock of a diagnosis and the weakness caused by treatment may make it difficult for her to accomplish basic daily chores. Offer to pick up groceries, drive the kids to soccer, or walk the dog. She may not have the energy for the necessities of life.

+ Suggest joining a support group.
Having people in her life that are going through a similar battle is an invaluable resource. It is important to feel like someone knows what she is going through. Other women fighting cancer can share their knowledge, resources, and support from a perspective that she will be able to connect to. They can be located on the Web, through a doctor, and through hospice care.

+ Use humor.
It is true that laughter is the best medicine. Laughing has been shown to increase immune functioning and allow momentary relief from the weight of the situation. Laughing does not mean that the situation is not dire, but it can help relieve stress. Always let your friend take the lead. Don't assume that she will find her hair loss funny, but if she makes a joke, feel free to laugh along.

+ Encourage her to take an active role in her recovery.
Cancer can create feelings of helplessness. Help the woman take as much control back as possible by encouraging her to be involved in her treatment. She can choose her health care providers, become educated about treatments, and practice self-care.

Counseling Tips

As your friend continues to progress through her recovery, encourage her in the following ways:

+ Help identify areas of her life where she does have choices.

Empower her to make as many choices as possible on her behalf. Help her identify the areas where she does have some control. She has control over her treatment, her perspective, her education about cancer and treatment, and she can make personal decisions that will affect her state of mind. She can also be involved in making end-of-life decisions, if necessary.

+ Deal with the anxiety and fear of the unknown.

Feeling afraid of the unknown is common to everyone. Cancer creates a situation with many unknowns, causing a continuous state of anxiety. Help her work through this by clarifying what is happening in the present moment. Help her learn relaxation techniques such as deep breathing, and practice them with her. Encourage her to voice her fears—they have less power after they are identified and brought out into the open.

+ Identify strengths.

Your friend will need to rely on her strengths in this time of crisis. Help her remember and focus on what she can still do, and do well, even with cancer. Facilitate her recognition of how these skills have helped in the past and how she can apply them to the current situation.

+ Discuss death.

Death is not something we openly discuss in our culture, but must be faced by all of us eventually. If the situation warrants, help her make choices about the end of her life while she is still able to do so. Let her speak openly about her death. Encouraging her to rely on her faith at this time will bring her comfort.

WHEN TO REFER

+ Suicidal thoughts

Fear of a painful or drawn out death may cause some to begin planning their own death. If the woman has mentioned harming herself or not having a reason to live, make sure she is safe and help her find a professional counselor immediately.

+ Depression

Feeling depressed is a normal reaction to a cancer diagnosis. If she seems to be overwhelmed by her depression she may need more intensive therapy.

SCRIPTURE HELP

+ **Joshua 1:6-9**
+ **1 Chronicles 16:8-36**
+ **Psalm 13**
+ **Psalm 103**
+ **Proverbs 3:5-8**

+ **Isaiah 40:25-31**
+ **Habakkuk 3:16-19**
+ **Matthew 5:3-10**
+ **Ephesians 3:14-21**
+ **Philippians 4:4-9**

Group Tips

+ Offer specific help.
Offer to drive her kids to school, or bring dinner over once a week. She will be more likely to accept help if you are clear about what you can do.

+ Let her share her story.
Listen as the woman tells her story without jumping in to tell about your friend, colleague, or parent who fought cancer. That takes the focus away from her and may not be helpful. Fight the urge to share your stories and make an effort to listen to hers.

+ Show continued support.
Often people make a big effort to be supportive when the woman is newly diagnosed and then forget about her long before her treatment is finished. She will need support all the way through her journey and after she has recovered. Continue to ask about her treatment and feelings about her illness.

+ Organize an informational meeting.
Almost everyone knows someone who has been impacted by breast cancer. The women in your ministry will be more prepared to help others if they know the specifics. Arrange for a guest speaker to attend your next meeting to talk about breast cancer and treatment. Encourage women who have been diagnosed to help organize the event, if they're up to it, and find out if there are any specific topics they want covered.

+ Offer to go to a doctor's appointment.
There is often a lot of information given at the doctor's office. If the woman is not feeling well or is emotionally distraught she may be unable to process all of the information, make decisions, or ask appropriate questions. Having support will make the process go more smoothly.

What Not to Say

+ "Did you know Sarah just died of that?"
We all know people who have died of cancer. At this time, though, it's not helpful to focus on death, but rather on life and a positive attitude toward what lies ahead. The same applies for asking insensitive questions such as when her hair will fall out or if she's heard of Betty's terrible experience.

+ "Set some goals and you'll live to see them."
While setting goals does give people a reason to take positive forward steps, this may seem flippant or shallow to someone faced with a myriad of medical and family related issues. If there is something important on the horizon, help her make plans toward that goal.

+ "Where's my anointing oil?"
While this is biblical and sometimes is just what is needed, be sensitive to the timing. There's a big difference between what is said between two close friends and making a public announcement in a crowd.

+ "My friend/mom/banker had breast cancer, and she... "
Unsolicited stories are rarely helpful. Don't forget that the woman has probably been bombarded with stories from many people and is most likely tired of hearing about everyone's relatives who did or did not survive. Instead, mention that you have walked through this with someone else and would be happy to help if she needs it.

What to Say

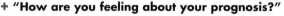

+ "How are you feeling about your prognosis?"
Asking about her feelings and truly listening to her response allows her to

express herself. Your sensitive response and listening ear can be a salve for worry, pain, and fear.

+ "I'll be right over!"

Pick up some food and go. Listen. Ask questions that help her think through her next steps. Get on the Web and look for helpful information with her. Ask what would be most helpful and do those things. Offer to go with her to appointments if you can.

+ "You can do this!"

Give strength and support. Breast cancer is very survivable, so offer hope. The word *cancer* strikes fear in all of our hearts. Be the one to dispel the fear and replace it with courage.

+ "I'll keep you in my prayers."

This is a beautiful and simple way to show her that you care. The woman's faith will be very important during her cancer. Knowing that others are praying for you is strengthening. If you say you're praying, be sure you are! Pray for her strength and for wisdom. Pray for her family, too.

+ "I am here for you."

Let her know that you will be there for her as she battles her cancer. Don't forget to provide continued support throughout the duration of her treatment and beyond. Just knowing there are people around who she can rely on will help her get through this time.

ADDITIONAL RESOURCES

+ Books

Counseling People with Cancer. Jann Aldredge-Clanton. Louisville, KY: Westminster John Knox Press, 1998.

Man's Search for Meaning. Viktor E. Frankl. New York, NY: Simon & Schuster, Inc., 1984.

Breast Cancer? Let Me Check My Schedule. Jo An Loren and Peggy McCarthy (Eds), Erma Bombeck (Author). Boulder, CO: Westview Press, 1997.

"Beating Breast Cancer." Ebony October 2002. Joy Bennet Kinnon and Zondra Hughes.

+ Online Resources

www.Komen.org (Susan G. Komen Breast Cancer Foundation)
www.cancer.org (American Cancer Society)
www.cancer.gov (National Cancer Institute)
www.mayoclinic.com (Mayo Clinic)

IMPORTANT FACTS

ABOUT BREAST CANCER

+ There are approximately two million women living in the United States who have been treated for breast cancer.

+ The chance of a woman having invasive breast cancer some time during her life is about one in eight.

+ The chance of dying from breast cancer is about one in 33.

CHAPTER TWO

Depression
Being There for Your Friend in the Darkness

with counseling insights from
REBEKAH KNIGHT-BAUGHMAN, PH.D.
+ ministry tips from **AMY WEAVER**
& CHRISTINA SCHOFIELD

I've always had a personality susceptible to depression. Depression isn't a sign of personal weakness or a condition that can be willed or wished away, despite what many people think. People like me who struggle with depression can't simply "pull themselves together" and get better.

The first time I experienced a deep depression, I felt lost. I was dealing with issues I'd never dealt with before. I'd essentially lost my dad through a divorce, and the feelings surrounding that experience created the depression that plagued me. Those feelings of being lost and alone were compounded when I lost the support of my mother and sister—I moved across the country to go to college and I became a Christian—two things they really didn't like. I felt abandoned when I needed support the most.

It was during that first year of college when I realized I had a serious problem. That was when I started failing…for the first time in my life. I'd always been successful in everything I did—I was an A student in school, a star on the track team, the editor of my school yearbook. But I just couldn't make myself do any of it anymore, and it wasn't long before I was on academic probation. Sure, I was discouraged about school, but it wasn't enough to get me out of the slump I'd sunk into. Eventually, I just stopped going to classes. Everything seemed like too much work.

My sophomore year of college, I promised myself I'd do better in school. But before the semester even began, I felt those familiar thoughts creeping in. I was overwhelmed before I even started. I felt unworthy of another chance, unworthy of love. I felt sorry for myself, like things were unfair and like nobody around me understood how I felt. I needed to know I was loved, so I tried to draw attention to myself. I tried to be funny, spiritual, encouraging—anything to get people to acknowledge me. It didn't last long—the effort was too much. So in the end, I just started avoiding people.

During this time, I didn't sleep or eat for days. And then at other times, I slept or ate way too much. It was a case of extremes. I cried a lot and then felt numb. I didn't want to bathe or get out of bed for days on end. I wrote in my journal that I wanted to be alone because no one understood me or knew what I needed. People felt fake. I wanted it all to go away. I felt helpless and hopeless.

I was a member of a small group in the women's ministry at my church. But for the most part, people in my small group didn't have a clue about what I was going through, and that hurt. Some people tried to fix me. When I didn't get better immediately, they either got frustrated with me or gave up on me. They told me I wasn't seeking God or I needed to try harder to get over my depression—as if all it would take was a simple "attitude adjustment."

But that wasn't everyone. There were those who were there for me. They listened to what I had to say. They sincerely cared about understanding what I was going through. They didn't simply offer quick fixes; instead they prayed for me and with me. They encouraged me by speaking truth into my life, writing notes, and showing me how important I was to them. Those unexpected gestures were done out of love, and they meant the world to me.

They pursued me when I thought I wanted to be alone. Getting out of my room and out of my bed was a positive thing, even if only to help me focus on something besides myself. When I said "no" to going places, they gently insisted. They told me they wanted me with them and expressed that I was important to them with their words and actions. It was what I needed.

And, really, it was those little things that got me out of the depression: prayer, love, meaningful actions, simple activities, a gift for no reason, an offer to watch my favorite movie, a listening ear, a special dinner made for me by special friends. God's love offered to me through God's people. They reminded me that God still loved me even if I didn't see him.

God worked through the people in my small group, and I gradually began to come out of my depression. It took time and effort on the part of the people around me. I started to take part in all the daily activities that I'd been avoiding, and my mood improved little by little. Some days were harder than others. And though I'll most likely always be susceptible to depression, I know that I have friends who will help me through it.

IMPORTANT FACTS

ABOUT DEPRESSION

✦ Nearly one in 10 adults each year are affected by depression—nearly twice as many women as men.

✦ On average, depression first appears during the late teens to mid-20s, though it can strike at any time.

✦ Almost all patients with depression gain some relief from their symptoms with treatment, and between 80 to 90 percent of people eventually respond well to treatment.

✦ About one in eight new mothers experience some degree of post-partum depression.

Care and Counseling Tips

THE BASICS

Depression is a dark and oppressive mood problem that can feel unbearable to the woman suffering from it. The burden of depression drags the person down as she tries to carry on with life as usual when life is not "as usual." Yet there is hope. By understanding the basic symptoms and causes for depression and learning to express care in ways that will be received well by the person who is depressed, you can share the burden of depression with your friend, and she will begin to feel the weight of depression lift. Look for the following symptoms if you think a group member may be depressed:

+ Emotional Symptoms of Depression

A depressed mood is usually characterized by hopelessness, sadness, discouragement, anxiety, and/or irritability all day, nearly every day for two weeks. These internal feelings may manifest in behaviors such as frequent crying, sharp and hurtful comments, a pessimistic outlook, and statements that reveal a sense of being overwhelmed by life.

+ Physical Symptoms of Depression

The body has a way of manifesting symptoms when a person is suffering emotionally. Depressed women may experience a change in appetite and in sleep patterns. In addition, depressed people tend to have several physical complaints and often take more trips to the doctor than usual.

+ Cognitive Symptoms of Depression

People who experience depression tend to think negatively about themselves. You may notice your friend making self-deprecating comments such as "You're a great leader. I could never lead without messing the whole thing up." Moreover, she may have difficulty thinking clearly, concentrating, or making decisions. If untreated, depression can lead to thoughts of death or, in the worst case, suicide. Be sensitive to comments such as "I just want to fall asleep forever," or "I can't go on like this anymore."

+ Behavioral Symptoms of Depression

Decreased energy, tiredness, and fatigue are characteristics of depression. You may notice that your friend's house has not been cleaned in some time, personal hygiene has declined, she is sleeping much more than usual, or she isn't enjoying things she normally loves.

+ Spiritual Symptoms of Depression

When a person is depressed, she may have a hard time connecting with God and believing in God's goodness and providence. Prayer may become difficult for her, as she may feel hopeless or guilty for not praying enough, in the right way, or about the right things. If the person's individual spirituality suffers during depression, corporate spirituality is likely to suffer as well. That is, she may have difficulty getting to church due to fatigue, and once at church, worship may be difficult.

+ Reasons for Depression

Most mental health practitioners agree that the combination of internal and external factors affect a person's mood. Here are some common influencers of depression:

- Genetic, biochemical, and hormonal factors
- Family history of depression
- Loss within relationship—death, divorce, or geographical relocation
- Feeling unsafe and insecure in relationships
- Change in employment status
- Dissatisfaction in work and/or work environment
- Negative thinking

Care Tips

When a woman is experiencing depression, it's difficult to know how to be present with her in the darkness. You want to let your friend know that you are caring and supportive, but you may feel drained by the heaviness and pessimism when you are with her. Here are some tips to help you serve your friend in her struggle to get out of depression:

+ Actively listen.
Encouraging your friend to talk about her sadness will foster understanding, which can help her feel a sense of control over emotions instead of feeling controlled by emotions. Although the feelings may frighten you, don't be afraid; just listen as you would to any friend of yours.

+ Spend time with your friend.
When a person is depressed, the natural tendency is to hide from others and try to recover on one's own. Your friend may be hiding because she is afraid of appearing weak or disturbed. But that's exactly the opposite of what is needed. A depressed person needs other people. Your presence will help shoulder the burden of depression, allow for rest, stave off loneliness, guard against suicide, and provide strength.

+ Suggest enjoyable activities.
Your depressed friend may not be able to come up with enjoyable activities due to a lack of excitement and joy. So share your joy. Suggest activities that she once enjoyed or those that you enjoy. Even if your friend seems resistant, there is a part of her that longs to do enjoyable things—it's simply buried under depression. Be persistent—human contact and enjoyable activities are good for her.

+ Exercise together.
It's a vicious cycle. The fatigue and lack of motivation caused by depres-

sion significantly impairs a depressed person's ability to exercise, but regular exercise has been shown to be a buffer against depression. You will be helping your friend immensely by committing to exercising regularly with her. Do it once a week, twice a week, or even once a day—any little bit will help. Play a sport, take an exercise class, or walk together after dinner.

+ Prepare meals.

When a friend is depressed, she may lose the motivation to cook and the desire to eat. Offer to prepare meals for your friend or cook together. The food and the fellowship will be invaluable.

+ Be nonjudgmental.

Depressed people judge themselves every day, so the last thing they need is a friend who judges them, too. Communicate patience and grace. By doing this, you may help your friend become more patient and gracious toward herself.

POSTPARTUM DEPRESSION

One of the most common and devastating kinds of depression for women is Postpartum Mood Disorder. All new mothers have a dizzying array of demands: a new life to care for; changing hormones; lack of sleep; body image issues; an altered social life. And to top it off, society says that a woman should be happy because she just experienced the miracle of birth.

For one in eight women, along with motherhood comes a very real, dangerous medical condition. About 80 percent of the time, postpartum depression goes undiagnosed and untreated. If you or someone you know is suffering with feelings of extreme depression, rage, irritability, anger, guilt, worry, feelings of inadequacy, or thoughts of suicide, speak with a medical professional or counselor right away. There's help available!

Counseling Tips

Many times depression calls for a professional counselor. Even so, there are many ways you can personally help counsel your friend through this tough time:

+ Build and maintain trust.

Trust takes time—it takes positive experiences built on more positive experiences. But once trust is built, it's easy to break—especially when things said in secret are later shared with others. As you counsel your friend, be sure to keep a policy of confidentiality—the *only* time you should talk to someone else is if your friend is abusing herself or another person.

+ Validate and normalize emotions.

Without crawling into the pit of depression with your friend, you can validate her emotions by expressing understanding and care. Normalizing depression can also help the person feel less alone in the process. By recalling another friend or family member who struggles with mood problems, you may bring the depressed woman a sense of relief that she is not the first or the last person to go through such a struggle.

+ Challenge faulty thinking.

Depression impairs people's thinking. Depressed people often feel unworthy of good relationships, success at their jobs, or a peaceful lifestyle. They often think that God has cursed them and that life is hopeless. If your friend expresses these feelings, gently challenge her, and speak the truth of God's love for her. Remind your friend that recovery from depression is a process, but it's treatable through professional counseling, fellowship, prayer, time, and medication if necessary.

+ Create positive affirmations.

Depression clouds the ability to think positively. One way to counter this is to help your friend come up with positive affirmations about herself. For instance, she may state, "I am treasured by God and worthy of love" or "I am a good artist." It doesn't matter if your friend wholeheartedly believes the affirmation or not, it will still serve as a reminder of who she is—a beloved creation and child of God. Encourage your friend to repeat the affirmations daily.

+ Trust God for your friend.

Don't be afraid to make mistakes. Trust God as you learn to care for and counsel your friend. Pray for your friend regularly, and ask God to give you wisdom and insight into your friend's heart.

ADDITIONAL RESOURCES

+ Books

Coping with Depression. Siang-Yang Tan and John Ortberg. Grand Rapids, MI: Baker Books, 2004.

When Someone Asks for Help: A Practical Guide for Counseling. Everett L. Worthington Jr. Downers Grove, IL: InterVarsity Press, 1982.

The Mother-to-Mother Postpartum Depression Support Book. Sandra Poulin. New York: Berkley Publishing Group, 2006.

+ Online Resources

www.nimh.nih.gov/publicat/friend.cfm (National Institute of Mental Health)

www.healthyminds.org (American Psychiatric Association)

www.suicidology.org (American Association of Suicidology)

www.dbsalliance.org (Depression and Bipolar Support Alliance)

http://outofthevalley.org/valley/links/default.aspx (Out of the Valley Ministries, Inc. - postpartum support)

Group Tips

A small group can be a *huge* source of support and strength to a woman struggling with depression. These tips will help your group minister to your friend:

✛ Talk about it.

Every person in a group influences every other person in the group. Together, identify ways in which the depression has influenced the group. Some people may notice that they're feeling depressed, frustrated, compassionate, or even angry. Take time to help people understand and empathize with the depressed person. As a group, talk about and research the dynamics of depression. Ask your depressed friend to share how she is feeling. Encourage others to share their own experiences with depression. Promote compassion, empathy, and knowledge within your group.

✛ Pray together.

Prayer can be one of the most important factors in fighting depression. Encourage your friend to share specific prayer requests during the group time. Pray together as a group, and also ask group members to pray daily for their friend.

✛ Show your support in fun, practical ways.

Create care baskets—Include cards, encouraging Scripture verses, herbal tea, music, movies, energy bars, gift certificates, and other fun things.

Regularly have group fun nights—Tailor them to your friend's liking by doing the things you know she used to enjoy.

Check in on the person—Organize a visit and phone call list that covers the person for a month at a time. Be sure that someone is either calling or visiting that person every day—especially in the early phase of depression. Once your friend has found a counselor and stabilized emotionally, the frequency of visits and phone calls could decrease to once per week.

Affirm your friend—Regularly send encouraging notes, "out of the blue" gifts, and funny e-mails. These will serve as reminders of your love and support.

+ Remember...

Reaching out to a person who is swimming in sadness and hopelessness is the best thing you can do. Don't give up—your efforts are making a huge difference.

WHEN TO REFER

+ When your friend becomes suicidal
If your friend expresses a desire to end her life, get help.

+ When your friend is a danger to others
If your friend expresses a sincere desire to harm another person, refer her to a mental healthcare worker, and notify the person whom she has plans to harm.

+ When a child is endangered or neglected
If your friend has children or works with children and she is unable to care for them, encourage the person to get help, offer to take the children for a time if you're able, or notify child protective services.

+ When your friend's daily functioning is impaired
Depression can impair a person's social, occupational, and personal functioning. If you know that she is not engaging socially, her work performance is suffering, or your friend is unable to get out of bed, feed, groom, and/or bathe herself, get help.

What Not to Say

✛ "As Christians, we should show the joy of the Lord."

This statement leaves no room for the spectrum of emotions common to the human experience. By making statements like this, you'll only cause your friend to feel further away from God than she already does. Your friend is probably aware that depression is not God's emotional design for anyone, and yet she still can't stop being depressed. As Christians, we should be human and show support and love when our sisters are struggling to find joy.

✛ "Stop being so negative, and look at the positive."

This statement may be said with good intentions, but looking at the good things in life isn't the answer for a person with serious depression. While negative thought patterns are one aspect of depression, it's a more complicated matter—depression isn't a choice and can't just disappear with an attitude adjustment. If your friend could simply "not be so negative," she would. Saying something of this nature would be like telling a blind person to not be so blind.

✛ "I know that you're better than this—don't give in!"

Saying this suggests that your friend is falling short and somehow failing to control her emotions. Your friend is likely already dealing with issues of self-worth and feelings of failure—this statement will only confirm those feelings.

What to Say

✛ "God is with you in this dark time."

By telling your friend this, you're reminding him or her of the relentless presence of God in all emotional states. You're telling the person that God is no stranger to depression and he won't leave or disappear when life is tough.

+ "How can I pray for you?"

With this statement, you're communicating that you wish to accommodate your friend spiritually as she journeys through this darkness.

+ "I love you."

Although this may seem too simple, when it's said often enough and demonstrated, it can make all the difference.

+ "If you ever need anything, I'm here. I'll call you on Friday to see how you're doing."

Someone struggling with depression has a hard time taking a first step with friends and needs to be pursued. Letting someone know you'll be there can be powerful. Be sincere, and then follow through on your words.

+ "I've been thinking about you today."

This statement reveals that you care. Follow it with thoughtful questions. Anything that shows you listened to a previous conversation and remembered what your friend said will demonstrate that you believe she is worth listening to and paying attention to.

+ "You're doing a great job with..."

Again, you're confirming that the person with depression is worthwhile, despite what she may be feeling. You're focusing on positive things even if she is incapable of doing so.

SCRIPTURE HELP

+ **Psalm 31; 32:1-7**
+ **Psalm 42:1-5**
+ **Psalm 139**
+ **Isaiah 40:29-31**
+ **Jeremiah 17:5-8**

+ **Romans 15:13**
+ **2 Corinthians 1:3-11**
+ **2 Corinthians 4:8-9**
+ **Ephesians 6:10-18**
+ **Philippians 4:4-8**

CHAPTER THREE

Divorce
Helping Your Friend Cope and Adjust

with counseling insights from **TERRI S. WATSON, PSY.D.**
+ ministry tips from **JOY-ELIZABETH F. LAWRENCE**

After almost 30 years of marriage, Maria made the difficult decision to file for divorce from her husband, Kevin. Although Maria believes that marriage is for life—through the good and the bad—Kevin had a history of marital infidelity and had not changed despite several years of counseling and church discipline.

Emergency Response Handbook: *How did your church respond to your divorce?*

Maria: The church called a congregational meeting since Kevin was the head elder. Kevin hadn't been attending the church for a while because of what was happening between us and because he traveled, which I'd used as a handy excuse when people asked where he was. Anyway, at the meeting the pastor said, "We called this meeting because we want to tell you that Kevin is under church discipline for moral failure." He asked the congregation to pray for my kids and me and also told them to address all questions to himself rather than to my family or me.

ERH: *How did your small group and Christian friends respond?*

Maria: There were times when I needed to talk about what I was going through, and this is what taught me who my friends really were. I had one friend who was really close, but she totally backed away. Another friend would talk about anything *but* what I was going through. Everything was all hush-hush and under wraps, but I didn't really want that. Also, when you're a couple and you do things with other couples and then are divorced, you don't get included in couple things anymore.

I did a Bible study together with a core group of female friends. Those ladies were my support group. They prayed for me diligently, and there was no way that I would have been able to walk that path and go through what I went through without them. I had seen other women go through divorce and wind up very angry, malicious, and ugly.

ERH: *How did you feel being a divorcing—and now divorced—Christian?*

Maria: Well first, there were the shame issues. That's a huge thing in Christian circles. I really had to work through that and was helped a lot by passages in Isaiah and Psalms.

Second, I was embarrassed—for what my husband had done, that I'd gotten myself in this situation, and that as a Christian I was going through divorce. Being divorced carries a stigma. Not that when I look at other divorced women I think of them badly, but it's hard being divorced. When you're a widow, there's definitely more sympathy. You don't choose to be a widow, but you have control over whether or not you're divorced.

I was angry, too, but I was careful of how and when I expressed it. I know that unwillingness to forgive slides a person into bitterness really quickly. But it was hard. I kept thinking, "This is horrific. This is my whole life. My married life was a lie."

ERH: *Do you have advice for others regarding forgiveness in the situation of infidelity and divorce?*

Maria: Forgiveness is a two-part thing. First, forgiveness isn't about the other person, it's about yourself. You have to let go of the right to retaliate, the desire to hurt him as badly as he hurt you. It doesn't happen all at once; it's a process that comes in stages—it ebbs and flows. There are layers to it like an onion. You get through one layer, then something will happen, and you'll have to peel the next layer.

Second, I had to understand that forgiving him didn't make what he did OK or mean that I condoned it. In the end I didn't forgive because of him, I forgave because it was a step of help for me. I told him, "As much as I know to this point, I forgive you."

ERH: *How would you summarize your experience of divorce?*

Maria: To me, divorce is a death. It's the death of a relationship. A lot of people will quote Romans 8:28: "And we know that in all things God works for the good of those who love him, who have been called according to his purpose" (New International Version). I don't believe that the divorce was "good," but I believe that "all things" means the big picture—everything, the bad and the good, rolled into one. It means that eventually God works it for good.

WHEN TO REFER

Most women going through a divorce can benefit from some professional counseling at some point in the process, particularly if they have children. Don't hesitate to encourage your friend to seek professional help immediately if any of the following signs and symptoms are present.

+ **References to self-destructive or suicidal thoughts or feelings**
+ **Isolating behavior**
+ **Continuous "bad-mouthing" of the ex-spouse in the presence of others, particularly the children**

Offering to sit with her during the initial call or accompanying her to an appointment can ensure that your friend receives the immediate help she needs.

Care and Counseling Tips

THE BASICS

A divorce is a vulnerable time for a Christian woman, but the love of Christ, expressed through Christian community, can make all the difference. Your ministry can offer Christ's love through competent and informed Christian caring, which involves understanding the many challenges, transitions, and effects of divorce.

+ Practical Concerns

Divorce causes dramatic changes in the woman's day-to-day tasks. She may need to secure a new place to live, take care of household tasks alone, maintain or seek employment, and manage finances.

+ Restructuring of Relationships

The effects of divorce are felt in nearly all of the divorcing person's relationships. Extended family may offer support, but relationships with in-laws can become strained. Some couple friendships are lost because many couples feel "caught in the middle" as they try to maintain friendships with both parties.

+ Emotional Effects

After the initial shock, divorced people often cycle through stages of anger, sadness, grief, and confusion before reaching a stage of acceptance in which they "move on" with their lives. Divorcing parents must also face the task of providing support and care for their children.

+ Spiritual Struggles

Following divorce, feelings of disillusionment toward marriage, the Christian life, and the church often create distance from God and make it difficult to trust him. Spiritual struggles are compounded by issues such as anger toward the ex-spouse and difficulties in forgiving. Some may also feel that God did not answer prayers for marital reconciliation.

Care Tips

The good news is your ministry can support women who are struggling with a dissolving marriage and adjusting to the changes that come along with divorce. Here are some practical tips for helping the women in your ministry.

+ Identify immediate needs.

When a group member discloses that she is going through a divorce, it's important to follow up to find out more about the circumstances. Don't be afraid to ask your friend to share immediate needs, such as the need for child care, financial help, or just a listening ear. Affirm your friend's courage in sharing those needs with others, and remind her that "bearing one another's burdens" is what Christian community is all about!

+ Be the "point person" in mobilizing the resources of the church.

Churches possess tremendous practical resources for a person going through a divorce. Coordinate the matching of church resources with areas of need that have been identified. Consult with your pastor to identify church members who can offer financial advice, legal counsel, child care, vocational guidance, and assistance in finding affordable housing. Offer to make the initial call to connect your friend with others who can assist in practical ways.

+ Utilize the resources of your ministry.

You need look no further than your women's ministry for resources that can be a tremendous support in the day-to-day practical challenges of a divorce. Practical ways for your group to help include providing child care, going with the person to court dates and legal appointments, connecting your friend with the local community college to explore vocational options, and initiating "nights out" on a regular basis to take your friend to a movie or dinner.

+ Offer information.

Knowing what to expect when going through a divorce can reduce anxiety, provide a greater sense of control, and normalize some of the difficult emotional components. Connect your friend with others in the church who have gone through a divorce. Provide her with information about a divorce support group in the community. Consider giving your friend a Christian self-help book on divorce (see additional resources below), and offer to meet together weekly to read and discuss. Anything you can do to offer information will help your friend tremendously!

ADDITIONAL RESOURCES

+ Books

The Fresh Start Divorce Recovery Workbook: A step-by-step program for those who are divorced or separated. Bob Burns & Tom Whiteman. Nashville, TN: Thomas Nelson, Inc. Publishers, 1998.

Helping Children Survive Divorce. Archibald D. Hart. Nashville, TN: Thomas Nelson, Inc. Publishers, 1997.

Successful Single Parenting. Gary Richmond. Eugene, OR: Harvest House Publishers, 1998.

When the Vow Breaks: A Survival and Recovery Guide for Christians Facing Divorce. Joseph Warren Kniskern. Broadman & Holman Publishers, 1993.

+ Online Resources

www.divorcecare.com
www.freshstartseminars.org

Counseling Tips

Helping the divorcing woman with the emotional, relational, and spiritual effects of divorce requires long-term involvement. This is a crucial ministry that can make a huge difference in the emotional and spiritual well-being of the woman and of her children. Here are some tips to help you as you counsel your friend.

✚ Listen actively and be nonjudgmental.

Meet with your friend on a regular basis, and make it your goal to actively listen. Encourage her to express fears, concerns, frustrations, and disappointments. Be empathetic and understanding. Resist the urge to "fix things" or give advice during these times—your task is simply to love! Be sensitive to the promptings of the Holy Spirit during these meetings. Be a good "sounding board" as your friend tries to negotiate the many tasks and challenges of a divorce. End your meetings together with prayer, and commit to pray specifically for your friend on a daily basis.

✚ Anticipate and plan for stressful transitions.

Going through a divorce is one of the most painful and stressful experiences an adult can face. You can be a tremendous help by assisting in the anticipation and planning for the many challenges of divorce. For example, what will it be like for your friend to see her spouse in court or to meet the new partner at one of the children's sporting events? Talking through these scenarios, practicing the desired response through role-playing, and anticipating times when extra support is needed are ways to normalize and manage the stress of these transitions.

✚ Help your friend assess her feelings toward her spouse.

The intense and conflicting feelings toward the divorcing spouse are a common place where people get "stuck" in the divorce process. Strong feelings toward her ex, if not worked through, can result in long drawn-out legal battles, damaging experiences for children, and a lifetime of bitterness. Providing your friend the opportunity to express and work through these feelings can be a tremendous source of support. Allow some degree of venting (better with you than with the children!). Discourage black-and-white thinking about the ex, such as "He's all bad" or "It's all his fault." Encourage forgiveness and "letting go."

+ Support healthy co-parenting.

When the divorcing woman has children, consider the needs of the whole family. Children's adjustment to divorce is significantly better if they can maintain good relationships with both parents. Encourage co-parenting, and be supportive of visitation and custody arrangements. Discourage "spouse bashing" in the presence of children. Encourage your friend not to rely on her children for emotional support but to develop the adult friendships available in your ministry. Be a friend to the children, and offer to connect them with additional sources of support.

+ Encourage your friend to have hope for the future.

With every crisis and loss, come opportunities for growth, ministry, and new and healthier relationships with God and others. At the right time, encourage your friend to focus on the possibilities available to her, and empower her to trust God for her future.

+ Don't be afraid to pray for reconciliation.

With God's help, your friends may eventually come back together again. Don't be afraid to hope for this!

Group Tips

Feelings of isolation, loneliness, and shame often keep divorcing Christians from utilizing the resources offered by a Christian community. Know that these feelings may make your friend drop out or disappear from your ministry during this difficult time—a time when she most needs that support. Reach out to your friend!

+ If the couple divorcing are both involved in your church, keep the following in mind:

It's very difficult for a church community when attempts to support reconciliation have failed and a couple chooses to pursue divorce. Feelings of failure, disappointment, and disillusionment can ensue and should be acknowledged. Everyone should be discouraged from taking sides—instead, they should continue to promote redemption of the situation by encouraging an amicable relationship: treating one another with respect, cooperating in co-parenting, and so on.

+ Provide a place to belong.

Offering a place of true belonging goes a long way in combating the feelings of isolation that are part of divorce. Be explicit in your commitment to walk through this difficult experience with the person. Watch out for—and discourage—judgmental or harmful comments toward your friend. Pursue your friend, even if she withdraws. And don't let your friend sit alone in church!

+ Offer a safety net for stressful times.

Sometimes the stress of divorce hits unexpectedly, and knowing there is a safety net of caring friends makes all the difference. Provide an index card with a list of names and numbers of ministry members whom the woman can call when in need of emotional support, child care, fellowship, or prayer.

+ Create a healthy, supportive group atmosphere.

As a group, commit to engage in honest acknowledgment of areas of sin and brokenness. Be accountable, confess your sins to one another, and actively promote forgiveness and reconciliation of differences. Seek to restore faith, hope, and love within your group. Remember, we can love each other only because God first loved us.

SCRIPTURE HELP

+ **Psalm 20**
+ **Psalm 27:1-3**
+ **Ecclesiastes 3:11**
+ **Isaiah 43:2-3**
+ **Romans 15:7**

+ **2 Corinthians 1:3-5**
+ **2 Corinthians 4:7-9**
+ **Philippians 2:12-13**
+ **James 5:7-8**

A "HEALTHY" DIVORCE

Although a divorce is rarely a welcome or positive experience in the life of a person, a "healthy" divorce is possible—one that minimizes the damage to the individuals involved, particularly if the couple has children. Recognizing the characteristics of healthy adjustment in divorce can help you provide competent, intentional caring as a woman in your ministry faces the difficult transition of divorce.

• Both parents remain involved with children in order to provide a continued sense of "family."

• Children are protected from the more negative impacts of divorce, including derogatory comments about the other parent.

• Both spouses are able to accept and integrate the divorce into their thinking about themselves and their future in a healthy way.

—taken from *The Expanded Family Life Cycle: Individual, Family, and Social Perspectives, Third Edition.* Betty Carter and Monica McGoldrick, Eds. Needham Heights, MA: Allyn and Bacon, 1999.

What Not to Say

Keep in mind that one of the worst things you can do is say nothing, which only intensifies the feelings of isolation and estrangement. When it's said in the spirit of true love and caring, even saying the wrong thing with good intentions is an act of caring. Here are some specifics to keep in mind:

+ "God hates divorce."

We need to love, not judge. Regardless of our views on divorce, broken relationships happen in the church due to the presence of sin in the world. When a woman in your ministry is going through a divorce, it's a time to show God's love, healing, and grace.

+ "It's not your fault."

Eventually, part of the process of healing involves recognizing, confessing and seeking forgiveness from God and the ex-spouse for one's own role in the breakdown of the marriage. Balance mercy and love with truth—don't discourage acceptance of personal responsibility.

+ "You've shared too much. I don't need to know that."

Most divorces are messy, and it's important to listen to someone when she needs to talk. Listen to the stories, even if it's hard for you. Besides, listening to your friend can help you assess where she is in the healing process and what she needs most right now.

What to Say

+ "I don't know what to say."

Don't avoid opportunities to talk to your friend, even though it may be uncomfortable for you to approach her. Be honest about your discomfort; this will put her at ease. Just be open to hear anything she wants to talk about.

+ "We're going to a movie on Saturday—want to come?"
After a divorce, many people are lonely. They miss the companionship that came with marriage. Sadly though, divorced people are often left out of social situations because they're not a pair. Don't let this happen! Invite your friend to dinner or a movie. If you're afraid he or she will be uncomfortable, *ask*.

+ "How are your kids doing?"
Ask if there is anything you can do to support the children of the divorcing couple. If you have kids of a similar age, arrange an activity for all of you to do together. This can be an opportunity to connect with your friend in a different environment, and can help you make sure the whole family is moving through the healing process.

+ "How can we help you this week?"
Do check in weekly with the person to identify specific areas of need, prayer requests, and anticipate upcoming transitions. It's often difficult for people to initiate asking for help during times of vulnerability.

IMPORTANT FACTS

ABOUT DIVORCE
+ According to a study by The Barna Group, 35 percent of married Christians have experienced a divorce, identical to the rate of non-Christians.

+ Nearly one-quarter of married Christians, 23 percent, get divorced two or more times.

+ According to The Barna Group, 52 percent of Christians disagree that divorce without adultery is a sin.

CHAPTER FOUR

Domestic Violence/Abuse
Intervening Before It's Too Late

with counseling insights from **TERRI S. WATSON, PSY.D.**
+ ministry tips from **LINDA CRAWFORD**

After 26 years of enduring an abusive marriage, Sarah finally made the difficult decision to change the future for herself and her children. Here is her story.

Emergency Response Handbook: *Did you know you were in an abusive relationship?*

Sarah: I didn't know that my marriage was abusive. There were things that happened along the way that should have been enormous red flags to me. But they weren't, probably because I had been raised as a child in an abusive home. What was happening in my marriage just looked like life to me.

ERH: *What was your childhood like?*

Sarah: My dad abused me sexually as a child. My mother was very physically abusive to me. If I did something or said something she didn't like she would grab whatever object was nearby and fling it at me. I grew up believing "If I do things perfectly then they'll love me."

Part of my upbringing was being part of this "perfect" family. I was supposed to think I was lucky to grow up in the family I grew up in. So as an adult I had my own "happy little marriage with happy little kids" and nobody saw what was going on behind closed doors.

ERH: *Share with us what happened in your marriage.*

Sarah: Larry was this big, broad-shouldered, take-charge kind of guy. He always had a good job, we had a beautiful home, and he came home every night. I thought that with all those good things my marriage couldn't really be that bad.

We had been married about six weeks when I remember our first big fight. I was curled up on the floor in the corner of the kitchen, and he was standing over me shaking his fist and yelling. But it didn't occur to me that it was wrong, because that was the way I had lived my whole life.

Larry was also very controlling. I had to account for every dime I spent and was not allowed to buy groceries because I spent too much. He had this philosophy that there were two ways to do everything—his way and the wrong way. He told me I was lazy, worthless, selfish, and uncaring. He would line up our two kids and me on the couch and stomp back and forth shaking his fist at us and yelling, "If you three people would straighten up and do what you need to do the way you need to do it, then this family will be fine. If you don't, then I'm out of here."

He was abusive outside our home, too. Early in our marriage Larry was arrested for making violent harassing calls to young women. I had people call and ask me, "Why are you staying with this man?" I said, "He's my husband, and it's my fault he did it." After that I did whatever he wanted, whenever he wanted, to keep him from hurting anyone else. I realized later through counseling that having sex when you don't want to, but are afraid not to, is called rape. Even in the context of a marriage. And this was a fairly regular occurrence.

ERH: *How did you begin to recognize you were in an abusive relationship?*

Sarah: I finally ended up in and out of psychiatric hospitals for two years. My husband's instructions to the staff when I was admitted were to "keep her until she's fixed." I had become suicidal because I was this good little Christian girl who believed you were married forever—until death do you part.

We tried couple's counseling six different times, but the agenda was always to find out what was wrong with me. Honestly, I didn't even know what the issue was then. The first time one of the doctors mentioned something about Larry, I thought, "What does he have to do with anything?" I believed I had a pretty good handle on things but finally came to understand that, if I didn't leave the relationship, I was going to die.

ERH: *Why do you think it was so difficult for you to get out of this abusive relationship?*

Sarah: I had a lot of fear. I had been forced to leave a very good job, and I was afraid of the financial situation. I had never really survived on my own. I was afraid to stay, and I was afraid to leave. I was afraid of how he would respond if I filed for divorce. I was afraid for my kids. There were a lot of kids' parents getting divorced and we used to tell ours, "Don't worry, we won't get a divorce—we are a family."

ERH: *What made you finally decide you needed to end the relationship?*

Sarah: I think I only came to that point after I connected with a battered women's shelter. I worked one-on-one with a lady for a couple of months, and she finally helped me to understand that what was happening in my home was not OK. My real healing started when I began working with a wonderful pastor at the church. I began to realize that what I had was not a marriage—not the way God describes a marriage.

ERH: *How did people respond when they found out you were getting divorced?*

Sarah: I was sure my daughter would be devastated when I told her, but she said, "Mom, thank you, when are we moving?" My son said, "It's about time."

Most people were in shock. We had this seemingly perfect little family. We lived in a brand-new house and I drove a nice car. One of my family member's first comments was, "How can you do this and leave this house?" There were very few people that knew what was really going on.

I had asked God "What am I supposed to do?" and I firmly believed that God was leading me out of the marriage. But that was not a very popular opinion. Many people in church felt that God would *never* end a marriage.

ERH: *Did you have women friends to support you?*

Sarah: At that time I really didn't know what friends were. I didn't know how to connect with anybody. I had women acquaintances, but none of them were friends who knew what was going on in my life. I lived on a superficial level and would just tell everyone that everything was fine and I was great.

One of the things I could have used was a friend to let me know that it was OK to be just where I was. That it was OK to hurt and it was OK to be angry. I needed someone to encourage me in the healing process I was going through.

ERH: *Did you find support at church?*

Sarah: I was always "doing" when I was at church. I played the piano, taught Sunday school, or whatever was needed. At the little church I had been in we talked a lot about salvation, but we didn't talk very much about a personal relationship with God. At that point in my life, my relationship with God was pretty much in my head. I knew the things to say and what to do, and I believed if I performed them well enough then God would love me. A woman friend said to me one day, "Sarah, I'm sick of this, you're going to church with me." It was at that church I realized I didn't even know how to sit in a congregation, I was so used to doing something!

Our little church eventually closed, and I began attending my friend's church and got connected to a pastor for counseling. During one counseling session the pastor told me, "It's OK, God loves you right where you are." I realized I hadn't even wanted God to love me before, because it was only the people who loved me who had hurt me. That's when God really became a part of my healing. I started learning that all these things I thought were my fault really weren't and that God had a plan for my life and wanted a relationship with me.

Back when I was married, there wasn't a real Sarah. I would change into a different person depending on who walked in the door and what their needs were. But I am Sarah today, and I'm OK.

Care and Counseling Tips

THE BASICS

Domestic abuse is the use of physical or sexual violence, threats, emotional abuse, or financial control in an attempt to dominate a spouse or partner. Despite the fact that domestic violence is a crime, most women are fearful and ashamed to tell others that they are experiencing abuse. We need to be ready to assist these victims when they find the courage to acknowledge their abuse and ask for help. Group leaders can play a critical role by knowing the signs and symptoms of domestic violence, understanding the effects of this violence on women, and engaging in a courageous Christian response when a group member discloses their experiences.

+ Symptoms of Domestic Violence

Women of all different ages, cultures, level of education, socioeconomic backgrounds, and denominations can be victims of domestic violence. Strongly suspect domestic violence if your group member reports that her partner engages in any of the following behaviors: threatening to hurt her or the children; frequently putting her down in public; forcing her to have sexual relations; hitting, kicking, slapping, choking, or biting her; limiting her contact with friends or family; blaming her for his angry outbursts. More subtle signs of domestic violence may include these partner behaviors: controlling of finances, suspicion and false accusations, checking her whereabouts and phone records, use of intimidation, and treating her like a servant or possession.

+ Effects

Many victims of domestic violence work very hard to give the appearance of a perfect marriage and family life. Underneath this brave façade, however, they experience symptoms of anxiety and depression. They have low self-esteem and feel a sense of shame and humiliation. It can be difficult for them to trust others, and they may be isolated and alone. Battered women have greater health and even reproductive problems, and are at risk for substance abuse. They may feel spiritually alone, adrift, and cut off from God and from Christian community, and confused about Christian views of marriage.

+ A Christian Response

Domestic violence is a frightening reality, even in the Christian community. We can be tempted to deny the existence of violence in Christian homes or to blame the victims. We feel hesitant to intervene in the private marital and family life of those in our congregation. However, it is imperative that the Christian response to domestic violence recognizes the reality of the problem and the biblical mandate to protect the innocent from violence by providing safety and healing for victims.

FOR THE BATTERER

If the abusive spouse or partner is also a church member, it is of critical importance that the church leadership holds him or her accountable for the abuse. The abuser should be removed from church leadership positions, confess the sin to those in positions of spiritual authority, and get professional help through enrolling in a domestic violence offender's treatment program. He or she should successfully complete the program, exhibit significantly changed attitudes and behaviors over a long period of time, and agree to ongoing accountability before steps toward reconciliation with the partner should be encouraged.

Care Tips

The initial disclosure of domestic abuse is a critical time when women are at highest risk for harm, as the batterer may make desperate attempts to maintain control of his partner and children. Competent pastoral care, professional help, and legal intervention can provide safety and hope for victims.

+ Support disclosure.

If you suspect a group member is experiencing domestic abuse, it is important to ask her directly. Express your concern for her safety and the safety of her children. Assure her that you believe her and that the problem is not her fault. Affirm that it is not God's design for her to continue to live in a violent relationship.

It is important to remember that domestic abusers will go to great lengths to maintain control of their partners and will attempt to discredit their partner's accounts of violence in the home. Many experienced pastors and mental health professionals have been fooled by convincing stories from the domestic abuser denying abuse in the home. Women rarely lie about domestic violence. It is better to err on the side of believing her and allowing others (the legal system, domestic violence specialists) to do the investigative work.

+ Put safety first.

Ensuring the safety of the group member and her children is the first priority. Provide her with information about domestic violence shelters in the community where she can receive housing, professional counsel, and legal assistance. The National Domestic Violence Hotline is a good place to start to find resources (1-800-799-SAFE). Reassure her that she is not breaking up the family by leaving, rather, her partner's violence has already "broken" the family. Offer her a place to stay in the interim while she makes the necessary arrangements. Protect her confidentiality and safety by keeping her whereabouts private.

+ Plan ahead.

Some women may disclose domestic abuse, but may not be ready to leave their abuser. It is important that friends and family members are supportive, nonjudgmental, and available during this time. Helping your group member develop a "safety plan" for her and the children is an important component of care. This might include helping her think through who she will call and where she will go the next time the violence escalates and encouraging her to begin to gather important papers, financial documents, credit cards, car and house keys, and personal items.

+ Provide resources.

Connecting your group member with key resources is an important next step. She may need legal help to obtain an order of protection. Referral to a support group for victims of domestic violence can help her begin to heal. She may need financial or employment assistance as she begins to establish greater independence. The National Domestic Violence Hotline can refer her to services in your community. The local phone book is a good place to find resources as well.

+ Offer spiritual counsel.

Your group member is likely to be experiencing significant spiritual confusion and in need of solid biblical perspectives on gender and marital issues. Domestic batterers often misuse Scripture to dominate their spouses and justify their actions. She will need your wise spiritual counsel to address erroneous beliefs. Reassure her of God's love for her (John 3:16), her value in his eyes (1 Corinthians 3:16-17; Psalm 139), and his desire for her to live in safety (Matthew 10:28-31; Romans 12:18).

Counseling Tips

Once the "secret" of domestic violence in a home has come out, the journey to healing can begin, and the church can play an important role in this process as the victim is supported and the batterer is held accountable for his actions. Your group member, and possibly even her partner, can be restored to personal and spiritual wholeness and healing, even if the relationship cannot be saved.

+ Address feelings of doubt, guilt, and shame.

Your group member's struggles with self-esteem are likely to manifest through negative statements about herself and her ability to manage the challenges before her. Empathize with her feelings and communicate your support and confidence in her ability to take steps toward self-protection and independence.

+ Help her be strong, patient, and let the Holy Spirit work.

Any significant changes will take time, patience, support, and much prayer. Help her set up the "necessary ingredients" for growth and healing, which can include spiritual mentoring, domestic violence support groups for her and the children, and possibly professional counseling. Encourage faithful and patient participation in the healing process.

+ Help her mourn the loss of the relationship.

Once she and her children are safe, she may begin to grieve the loss of the relationship she once had with her partner that was brought to an end by his violent behavior. Listen, support, and encourage her to mourn this loss. If the batterer has refused to acknowledge his wrongful actions and participate in treatment, she will need to let go of the relationship for her safety and the safety of her children. Remember, it was his violence that ended the relationship, not the choices she has made to protect herself.

Group Tips

Showing the love of Christ through caring action can help the domestic violence victim negotiate the many challenges she faces in creating a place of safety for herself and her children.

+ Go with her.
Your friend is likely to feel alone, afraid, and insecure as she takes steps towards self protection and independence. Christian friends can be an invaluable resource for the support and companionship she may need. Develop an "on call" schedule with names and phone numbers of group members she can call on a daily basis to go with her on errands, appointments, support group meetings, even school or sports functions with her kids where she may encounter her partner.

+ Protect her privacy.
Her safety and the safety of her children may depend on this. If she has left her battering spouse and is staying at a shelter or with friends, do not reveal her whereabouts to anyone.

+ Provide comfort and support.
Remember, she has been and may be still going through a traumatic experience comparable to living in a "war zone." Let your group be a safe haven of support, and nurture. Care for her through providing comforts such as meals, Christian CDs, and notes with prayers or passages of Scripture. Pray with her regularly for safety, protection, and healing.

+ Encourage outside activities.
If your friend is still with her partner, she is at risk of becoming increasingly isolated from friends and outside involvement as he attempts to take more control of her life. Encourage her to stay involved with friends and with church activities, offer to pick her up for events, and initiate social

involvement with her on weekends. Help her to stay involved despite pressures from her partner to the contrary.

+ Recognize your limitations.

Once you hear about a battered friend's experience, it is normal for you to want to help and protect her and her children from further abuse. It is important to remember that you cannot "rescue" her. She needs to be ready to take the necessary steps towards safety herself. Many women go though numerous cycles of violent behavior, apology, and reconciliation before they are able to take action to remove themselves from the abusive home environment.

ADDITIONAL RESOURCES

+ Books

No Place for Abuse: Biblical and Practical Resources to Counteract Domestic Violence. Catherine Clark Kroeger and Nancy Nason-Clark. Downers Grove, IL: InterVarsity Press, 2001.

Why Does He Do That? Inside the Minds of Angry and Controlling Men. Lundy Bancroft. New York, NY: Berkley Publishing Group, 2002.

+ Online Resources

www.peaceandsafety.com
www.focusministries1.org
www.ndvh.org (National Domestic Violence Hotline)

What Not to Say

+ "If you had told me, I could have helped."

Most women in abusive relationships are not able to reach out for help, and may keep friends at a distance on purpose. Saying this implies that it was her fault that you were not able to be there to help. The last thing she needs now is to feel guilty for failing in your friendship. Move on from what was happening before—help now.

+ "Maybe if you..."

Comments about what she could do differently at home to stop her husband's violent behaviors only reinforce what she fears most: If she were a better wife, he would not be this way. That is simply not true. The decision to be violent is his alone. She did not cause the domestic abuse, nor can she stop it by changing her behavior. Only his acknowledgment of his problem and willingness to seek professional help will stop the violence.

+ "Do you really want to break up your family?"

It is the violent behavior of the partner that has broken the family, not the battered wife's decision to leave to protect herself and her children.

+ "Try marital counseling."

Once a partner has resorted to violent behavior, marital counseling is not an appropriate recommendation and may even result in greater harm. He first needs to successfully complete a program specifically designed to treat domestic batterers. Only then, with the recommendation of professionals, should marital counseling be attempted.

+ "Forgive him and give him another chance."

Words of apology are insufficient evidence that a batterer has truly repented of his abusive behavior. Confession, accountability, participation in domestic violence counseling, and changed attitudes and behaviors over an extended period of time will demonstrate true repentance. This level of change takes time and may require a period of marital separation. Encourage her to seek professional input in assessing whether lasting change has occurred.

What to Say

+ "I'm so sorry you had to live through that."

Validate your friend by acknowledging the amount of pain she must have been through; then help her move forward into healthier relationships. Women who have been in abusive situations need relationships with women who have strong healthy marriages and friendships. When she sees that a marriage can be full of love and mutual respect, it will give her hope that it is possible to have a different life than the one she has known.

+ "I'm here to listen."

You don't have to have the answers. Most women coming out of an abusive relationship are so overwhelmed that they don't even know there are answers. More than likely she is not accustomed to confiding in anyone and it will take time for her to build trust in your friendship. Be prepared to make the commitment to be a friend who will care enough to just sit and listen, and listen some more.

+ "Are you OK?"

If you suspect that a group member may be experiencing domestic violence, ask her. Let her know what you have observed and what your concerns are. Be persistent in your caring. Let her know that you believe her and want to be there to help.

+ "It is not your fault."

Your group member needs to hear this message over and over again. Domestic abusers often convince their partners that the abuse is their fault. Her behavior did not cause the violence; it was his choice to be violent and he is the one who needs to change. Gently challenge her assumptions that she can change him by her words or actions.

✛ "Let us walk with you through this difficult journey."

She needs to know that you are willing to be an ongoing support as she figures out what steps she needs to take and starts on the path toward healing and wholeness. Remind her that you want to meet with her on a regular basis for prayer and support.

IMPORTANT FACTS

ABOUT DOMESTIC VIOLENCE

✛ During an average year, four million American women experience a serious assault by a partner.

✛ For 30 percent of women who experience abuse, the first incident occurs during pregnancy.

✛ Some estimates report almost one million incidents of violence occur each year against a current spouse, former spouse, boyfriend, or girlfriend.

SCRIPTURE HELP

✛ **Deuteronomy 31:8**
✛ **Psalm 27:1**
✛ **Psalm 31:19-20**
✛ **Psalm 37:5-6**
✛ **Psalm 57:1**

✛ **Psalm 91:14-16**
✛ **Psalm 139:1-18**
✛ **Jeremiah 29:11**
✛ **Matthew 11:28-30**
✛ **Philippians 4:13**

WHEN TO REFER

+ Provide her with resources in the community

If a woman in your ministry is experiencing domestic violence, your first concern needs to be her safety. Give her the National Domestic Violence Hotline number at 1-800-799-SAFE. Give her the numbers of local domestic violence shelters, hotlines, and support groups. Help your group member obtain temporary housing for herself and her children, legal counsel, financial assistance, and counseling services through a local agency.

+ Encourage her to consider professional counseling

Counseling services with a certified domestic violence counselor can be an important part of her healing. If your group member expresses suicidal or homicidal thoughts, evidence of substance abuse, isolation and withdrawal, and an increase in symptoms of anxiety and depression, it is imperative that she receive professional help.

+ When to act immediately

If your friend calls you in the midst of a domestic dispute and you fear for her safety, do not hesitate to call the police. Sometimes legal involvement is a necessary first step toward addressing the problem.

If you have a reasonable suspicion that children are experiencing abuse, a report must be made to National Child Abuse Hotline. The national number is 1-800-4-A-CHILD.

CHAPTER FIVE

Eating Disorders
Helping Create a Healthy Relationship With Food

with counseling insights from **LAURA GREINER, PH.D.**
+ ministry tips from **AMBER VAN SCHOONEVELD**

Disorder is such an unpleasant word, one I certainly don't want to associate with. But we're all on a continuum in our relationship to food and eating. On one end, there are healthy behaviors and thought processes. On the other end...well, you know.

I spent my first year of marriage in a nice, comfy spot on that continuum. Definitely in the honeymoon phase, my husband and I plunged ourselves into enjoying life together (including lots of tasty Dairy Queen treats). The outcome? A *really* fun first year of marriage...and 20 extra pounds coating my body.

My weight has always yo-yoed. I'd gain 10 pounds, then exercise it off, then gain and lose again. So this gain was no biggie; I'd just work it off again. I started a diet and fitness program, and at the end of 12 weeks, I had lost 12 pounds. I was so proud.

So I decided to lose some more. I got down to my pre-marriage weight and was elated. Each time I stepped on that scale in the morning, I was rewarded with those happy, falling numbers. Step on. Ding! You've lost one pound. The feeling was so good; I decided to lose more. Ding! Two more pounds...five more pounds...10 more pounds. Those numbers became my drug. Like one of Pavlov's dogs, each time I heard the ding of the scale turning on, my mouth would salivate, waiting for the treat of self-affirming achievement. The numbers that eluded me even in high school were now obliging me with a visit.

Then I hit the jackpot. Size 4. What a beautiful little number. Like a cocaine addict, I drowned in its pleasure and wanted more. I reached deeper in for more discipline—exercising six days a week, sometimes twice a day, and eating only small meals.

But something happened. One day I stepped on the scale for my fix. Whether conspiracy of the universe or simple water weight gain (I suspected the former), the scale moved up one pound. Don't panic. Next week: two pounds.

And here's where I broke.

Like a junkie denied my drug, I flipped. Those two pounds, so small and innocent, became my universe. The world stopped and hinged on this one fact: I *must destroy* those two pounds.

With all the self-discipline in my soul, I threw myself into weight loss, obsessed with eating as little as possible. As I sat at work in my cubicle, I'd think, *"Cheese stick, 11 o'clock. That should last me at least three hours. Next food: apple, 1 o'clock."* I wished secretly for the discipline of an anorexic.

But I was fooling myself—I loved food and I loved eating. And so, my obsession with *not* eating very smoothly transitioned to an obsession with eating. When could I eat next? What would I eat next? Before the morning snack was swallowed, I would calculate how to pass the time until my next feeding. My snacks became more frequent…and more sugary…and more chocolaty.

The drug of food replaced that of the falling numbers on the scale. The numbers had conspired against me, glaring up at me each morning, defying me to defeat them. I couldn't. All I had left was me and the food—the food that had so cruelly caused this unthinkable gain and the food that became my constant companion in my rage against the scale.

Then came the shame. *I blew it again. I'm worthless. I deserve to be punished.* Like many who struggle with compulsive overeating, I would follow what I considered ultimate failure with punishment—forcing myself to eat yet more, thinking, *"I deserve to fail and be overweight."*

Then one day on the way to work, I woke up. I had packed my daily food as always: a protein bar, a cheese stick, a sandwich, a cookie. While driving, I obsessed over my eating for the day—the when's and what's. And as I pulled into the parking lot, I noticed. An empty protein bar wrapper. An empty cheese stick wrapper. An empty bag where the cookie had been. Still full from too much cereal at breakfast but so focused on not eating, I'd eaten the entire contents of my lunch on the way to work in one large gulp. And I woke up. *"A protein bar? Who binges on a protein bar? They don't even taste good! In fact, I hate protein bars. I'm a mature, intelligent adult... I think. This is definitely not normal."*

I realized I had to tell someone. I had become an angry, insensitive person obsessed with food. I didn't want this to define and destroy me. So I told a friend. Then I told my husband (asking for his forgiveness for trampling him in my rampage). I went to the library and checked out some books on compulsive overeating, desperately hoping the librarian wouldn't notice the titles as she checked them out.

I found out about a 10-step program for those who compulsively overeat, and I began the healing process. I learned that I fit so many of the characteristics of those with compulsive overeating disorder, eating when not hungry without enjoying it, thinking constantly about food, feeling out of control when around food, having feelings of guilt after overeating, punishing myself for failure.

I was lucky. My protein bar binge woke me up to my abnormal behavior, and I sought help before I was caught in a years-long battle. But I could have stayed on that roller coaster; millions do.

Sitting across from my trusted friend, telling her that I couldn't stop eating, that food was all I could think about, I felt about 3 years old...ashamed, embarrassed, and guilty. But I found love, acceptance, and understanding. She promised to listen to me whenever I needed her, and not to judge. Having a fallback person to call when the fingers started twitching for a binge somehow diminished the control food had on me—it wasn't just me and the food anymore.

Care and Counseling Tips

THE BASICS

An eating disorder is a complex psychological condition that manifests itself in unhealthy eating behavior. There are three primary eating disorders:

1. **Anorexia nervosa**—not eating enough food
2. **Bulimia nervosa**—drastic measures to rid the body of food including purging through vomiting, overuse of diuretic/laxatives, or excessive exercise
3. **Binge eating disorder**—repeatedly overeating in a short period of time

Eating disorders have serious emotional, social, and physical effects. Many people with eating disorders experience (either now or in the past) anxiety, depression, substance abuse, and childhood sexual abuse. Eating disorders can lead to serious physical problems including osteoporosis, damaged stomach, high blood pressure, heart problems, and death. And although eating disorders appear to be about preoccupations with food and weight, they are almost always about much more than food. Eating disorders are a complicated web of social, emotional, behavioral, and psychological factors, and they have multiple risk factors, causes, effects, and treatment strategies. Eating disorders can quickly spin out of control into a vicious cycle of personal destruction and they almost always require professional and group help.

✛ Symptoms of Anorexia Nervosa

- Avoiding food
- Eating only "safe" foods—low in calories and fat
- Having odd rituals such as weighing food or cutting food into small pieces
- Spending more time playing with food than eating it
- Cooking meals for others without eating

- Compulsive exercising
- Dressing in layers to hide weight loss
- Spending less time with family and friends and becoming withdrawn and secretive
- Fatigue, irregular heart rate, brittle nails and hair, low blood pressure

✛ Symptoms of Bulimia Nervosa

- Taking repeated trips to the bathroom, especially after eating
- Compulsive exercising
- Taking diuretics or laxatives after eating
- Becoming secretive about food and/or spending a lot of time thinking about and planning the next binge
- Stealing and/or hoarding food
- Dehydration, fatigue, constipation, damaged teeth and gums, irregular heartbeat

✛ Symptoms of Binge Eating Disorder

- Eating alone
- Eating very quickly
- No control over eating behavior
- Consumed with self-dislike and guilt
- Fatigue, joint pain, increased blood pressure and/or cholesterol

Care Tips

+ Express concern.

If you are concerned that a woman in your ministry has an eating disorder it is important to express your concerns. You will want to find a private place where you can talk to her in a loving and supportive way. The earlier you express your concerns the better.

+ Be specific.

In a calm and caring way, say specific things you have noticed which have caused you to be concerned. For instance, you might say, "I have noticed you usually don't eat with the group, and the few times you have joined us you have excused yourself to the bathroom immediately after eating."

+ Assess the bigger picture.

Often, the beginning of an eating disorder in a woman's life is triggered by a stressful life event, which can lead to weight loss. Looking at what is going on in the woman's life can be a helpful tool in talking with her about the eating disorder.

+ Get more help.

After talking with the woman, if you are still concerned about her health and safety, it is a good idea to talk with the woman's family and/or a trusted health care professional to discuss intervention possibilities.

Counseling Tips

+ Avoid "you" statements.
Try to use "I" statements as much as you can in order to avoid placing shame, blame, and guilt. For instance, you would want to say, "I am concerned about you" instead of "you really need to eat."

+ Provide continued support.
Whether the woman with the eating disorder is ready to deal with her food issues or not, it is important for you to communicate your continued support wherever she is on her journey.

+ Model healthy eating and lifestyle choices.
If you're dieting and focusing too much attention on losing or gaining weight, it may reinforce your friend's obsession. Instead, model balanced living that focuses on eating and being active for health's sake and for enjoyment rather than on weight or the next diet fad.

+ Recommend nutritional help.
Often women struggling with eating disorders need education about the nutritional value of food—particularly if they have lost track of what "normal eating" is. Suggesting that a woman meet with a nutritionist can be an excellent source of support and reinforcement of healthy eating behaviors. You could also offer to go with the woman to her first meeting with a nutritionist.

Group Tips

A group of friends can give a woman the support, encouragement, love, and sense of normalcy she needs to bolster her on her journey toward health.

+ Model balanced behavior.

If possible, have your group model good eating habits around and about food. It can help a woman with an eating disorder move toward healthy behavior and thinking habits. For instance, if your group has a potluck together you could agree to bring healthful dishes. But don't be afraid to occasionally enjoy a special treat together, like a special homemade dessert made by one of your women. This sort of balance around food can provide a woman struggling with an eating disorder with positive examples of how we are intended to use and enjoy food.

+ Avoid dieting discussions.

Dieting is a common trigger for eating disorders. What may start out as an attempt to lose a few pounds can turn into a dangerous eating disorder. Talking about diets and weight loss happens frequently among women—but if a woman in your group is battling an eating disorder this type of conversation may add fuel to the internal war that is already battling inside of her. Avoiding "diet" talk is a good rule of thumb.

+ Replace lies with truth.

A great group exercise is to discuss different "lies" that women in the group have bought into—and then replace those lies with a biblical truth. Talking about where the lies came from and how they affect our lives is an important piece of the discussion. A few examples of lies include:

"I am not lovable."
"My worth is based on what I accomplish."
"I am not beautiful."

"I am beautiful only if I am thin."

Together you can look for and find Scripture to replace these lies. (Psalm 139:13-14 is a great place to start.)

+ Plan fun events that don't center on food.

Associate good times, relaxation, and comfort with activities other than eating by treating yourselves together with activities such as walking, shopping, getting massages, dancing, and so on. If your friend has certain triggers to binge eating, such as ice-cream parlors, find fun Friday-night alternatives such as trips to local art galleries or walking at a mall.

+ Be prepared for long-term support.

The road to recovery from an eating disorder can be long—potentially taking years. Pray to God for patience and hope, and tell your friend that you will support her for as long as she needs.

SCRIPTURE HELP

+ **Exodus 20:3**
+ **Psalm 34:4-8, 18**
+ **Psalm 103:1-5**
+ **Jeremiah 29:11-13**
+ **Romans 12:1-2**
+ **1 Corinthians 6:19-20**
+ **1 Corinthians 10:13-14**
+ **Philippians 4:13**
+ **1 Peter 1:13-15**

What Not to Say

+ "You're looking so skinny."
This may be an innocent observation, but you never know what is going through your friend's mind, and she may read far too much into it, being overly sensitive to her appearance and weight. Focus on health instead of weight.

+ "You look fine; just stop eating so much."
…Or "Just stop making yourself throw up," or "Just start eating." Avoid simplistic solutions and questions. Eating behaviors are extremely complicated and simple solutions can feel very defeating.

+ "You're going to eat *that*?!"
Don't reinforce the labels of "good" and "bad" food to those with eating disorders. The label is often then projected onto the person, resulting in a cycle of guilt when one has "been bad."

+ "I know how you feel…I really want to lose 15 pounds, too."
If your friend has an eating disorder, the problem goes further than just needing to gain or lose weight. This kind of relating will actually serve to make your friend feel further away from you because it's clear you *don't* really know how she feels—her disorder isn't just a passing desire to lose weight.

+ "I don't understand how you can make yourself throw up. Yuck."
Comments on behavior that is inexplicable to you makes the friend feel like an oddity and don't serve to build trust. Instead make comments that build solidarity, such as "I want to understand how you're feeling so I can know how to encourage you."

What to Say

+ "Thank you so much for talking to me."

Admitting her struggle to you was probably a very big step that took your friend a lot of bravery. She may be feeling very insecure after laying her struggles bare before you. Affirm her by acknowledging this brave and important first step.

+ "I am proud of you."

It can be very helpful in the recovery process to tell a woman with an eating disorder that you believe in her and are proud of her. Most women with eating disorders suffer from very low self-esteem, so providing them with specific things they are doing well can be uplifting and motivating.

+ "You can talk to me anytime about this struggle, and I won't judge you."

Shame, embarrassment, and guilt keep many women in the closet of their eating disorder. If a woman knows she can tell you about any of her experiences without losing your respect and encouragement, it will make her feel much less alone in the fight.

+ "I love you, and I think you're beautiful—and so does God."

Remind your friend that she is lovable, valuable, and worthwhile. It might seem like these messages don't get through at times, but don't give up reaffirming her.

+ "How can I support you?"

Regardless if the woman is dealing with her eating disorder or denying it, this kind of question feels nonjudgmental and comforting. It can also help her not feel so alone.

ADDITIONAL RESOURCES

+ Books

The Eating Disorder Sourcebook : A Comprehensive Guide to the Causes, Treatments, and Prevention of Eating Disorders. Carolyn Costin. Los Angeles, CA: McGraw Hill, 1999.

Lying in Weight: The Hidden Epidemic of Eating Disorders in Adult Women. Trisha Gura. New York, NY: HarperCollins, 2007.

God Hunger: Breaking Addictions of Anorexia, Bulimia, and Compulsive Eating, Desiree Ayres. Lake Mary, FL: Creation House, 2006.

+ Online Resources

www.edap.org (National Eating Disorders Association)

www.nlm.nih.gov/medlineplus/eatingdisorders.html (U.S. National Library of Medicine and National Institute of Health)

www.edreferral.com (Eating Disorder Referral and Information Center)

www.anad.org (National Association for Anorexia Nervosa and Associated Disorders)

www.womenshealth.gov (The National Women's Health Information Center)

www.harriscentermgh.org (Harris Center for Education and Advocacy in Eating Disorders)

IMPORTANT FACTS

ABOUT EATING DISORDERS

✚ In the United States, as many as 10 million women are battling an eating disorder, such as anorexia and bulimia (not including binge eating disorder).

✚ Four out of 10 people in the United States have either suffered or know someone who suffers from an eating disorder.

✚ Over half of teenage girls in America use unhealthy behaviors such as skipping meals, fasting, smoking, vomiting, and taking laxatives to control their weight.

WHEN TO REFER

✚ When a woman admits to an eating disorder

If your friend admits she has an eating disorder, you will want to refer her to medical and psychological professionals.

✚ When a woman denies an eating disorder

If a woman denies she has an eating disorder but you have reason to believe otherwise, consult with the woman's family as well as a mental health professional to see what steps to take next.

✚ Refer women with weight preoccupation to a dietician and/or nutritionist

If a woman does not have an eating disorder but shows risk factors such as obsessing over food and weight, refer her immediately to health care or nutrition professionals who can help redirect her behaviors and preoccupations with healthy thinking and behavior.

CHAPTER SIX

Empty Nest
Helping Your Friend Adjust to Family Changes

with counseling insights from **LAURA GREINER, PH.D.**
+ ministry tips from **HEATHER DUNN**

My first taste of an empty nest came when my son left for college. I couldn't take my eyes off him as he walked away and then disappeared around the corner of the campus building. He seemed so young and vulnerable. I so wanted him to be successful and not be homesick. Then, just three short years later, my daughter left, too. Though I had read books and talked with a friend, it was harder than I expected. It was like mourning a death—the death of the family I'd once known and hoped would last forever. I knew that e-mail and cell phones would allow me to contact my children, but not like I had before. Depression and sadness followed me for weeks as I daily faced my now empty-feeling house.

My husband, though caring, was involved in providing extra care for his ailing mother. So, I put on a good front for him, acting the part of a contented wife to alleviate extra stress for him. I was more alone than I could ever remember being.

Suddenly, there was plenty of time to ask questions like "Who am I?" How would I be defined now that I was no longer defined by my children? Would God have anything significant for me to do? Would God be there for me now? What would I do for fun? What would I talk about with my husband?

At first there was no immediate answer. I encountered self-pity in my loneliness. My kids weren't there. Neither was my husband. It didn't feel like God was there either. I began to realize how often God had been put in the back seat while I cared for my kids. I began putting aside special times on a weekly basis just to spend with God. Yes, I prayed for my family, but I also took time to praise God and just *be* before him. I began to see how God had been there all of the time; he'd been waiting for me to turn around and notice.

With new time in my schedule and the flexibility to make more choices about my time, I felt a little selfish at first. I both loved and feared the feeling that my world revolved more around me. I was used to continually putting my needs on the back burner. Now they were moving to the front! I joined a women's health club. I continued working part time.

I didn't just want to do the fun stuff, though. I wanted to find continued meaning and purpose for my life. I joined a women's Bible study with a friend. And, with persistence from an associate, I agreed to lead a high school girls' small group.

Within a year, my mother-in-law passed away. After the grieving and household details had been taken care of, my husband was more available. We began to reconnect in new ways. We spent more leisurely evenings and even had dates. I planned surprises for him and tried to give him my full attention in the evenings. We intentionally talked about many things in addition to our children.

I've had to work at some things. I've had to work at my relationship with my husband. I've had to work at cultivating friendships. I've had to work at letting my kids have the freedom they need to find their own wings. I've had to work at accepting my new role in my family.

Now, after almost two years, I've come to see that you can never be prepared for an empty nest, but you will get through it. There's sadness and there's joy. Every time the kids leave after a visit, the sadness returns. It doesn't last as long, but it's still there. There's joy every time they call or send an e-mail or ask for advice. There are old friends and new and time to spend with them, even spontaneously. My family still needs me. God still needs me. Life's not over but it is different. There's a whole new chapter unfolding!

Care and Counseling Tips

THE BASICS

The term empty-nest syndrome refers to an emotional condition some women experience when one or more of their children move out of the home. Many mothers have dedicated two decades to raising their children, so when their last child moves out of the home they may feel their primary and most meaningful role has ended. They may feel a deep loss, sadness, and loneliness. And, unlike grief over a death or loss of health, empty-nest grief is often overlooked because a child moving out of the home is seen as healthy and normal.

In many cases the empty-nest syndrome can be compounded by other life transitions such as menopause, retirement, or the stress of caring for an aging parent. Marriages can also be a source of stress with empty-nest syndrome. A couple who is used to having children around may find it a bumpy transition when it is just the two of them in their home.

✛ Symptoms of Empty-Nest Syndrome
• Abrupt and overwhelming emotions
• Depressed mood, sadness, crying
• Sense of emptiness and insignificance
• Feelings of guilt and regret over things done or not done with children

The empty-nest syndrome is most often experienced by women, but men can experience it as well. It can occur when a child goes to college but also again when a child gets married. Two factors that seem to particularly affect the empty-nest syndrome are the emotional closeness a woman has with her child and her working status. If the empty-nest mom spent a lot of time with the child who moved out and she does not work outside of the home, she may have a very difficult empty-nest adjustment.

Care Tips

+ Open the door for sharing.

A woman feeling the pangs of loneliness after her child moves out can find herself visiting the child's empty room, maybe rummaging through his/her drawers, and even picking up a T-shirt and inhaling the scent. This may be something she would never share with anyone because it would be too embarrassing. It is important for you to let your friend know her feelings are nothing to be ashamed of. Once your friend feels comfortable with you, encourage her to talk about her sadness and express her grief.

+ Double check.

Assess other factors in the woman's life such as marriage, stress levels, and physical health. If there are other issues going on you will want the woman to consider and care for these issues separately from her empty-nest emotions.

+ Get more help.

Some depressions provoked by the empty-nest syndrome can become very severe. Excessive crying, not wanting to socialize, and difficulty going to work may be important signs that something more then the empty-nest syndrome is going on. In this case encourage your friend to seek professional counseling.

Counseling Tips

+ Encourage support.
Encourage the woman to seek special support for this time of transition in her life. She needs people whom she can talk to on an ongoing basis and who can provide her with prayer and encouragement.

+ Encourage new growth.
Encourage the empty-nest mom to consider exploring things she has put on the back burner while she has raised her family. Maybe she has always wanted to take gourmet cooking classes, learn to play golf, or take a creative writing course. Encourage her to see this transition as a new era in which God can use and grow her in new and exciting ways.

+ Encourage self-kindness.
Women are often quick to find fault and be critical of themselves. Encourage your empty-nest mom to be easy on herself as she goes through this transition. Let her know it is important to allow herself to feel what she feels without beating herself up.

+ Encourage her to not wallow in regrets.
No mom is perfect. All moms make mistakes. It is important to let your empty-nest mom know that God is bigger than her mistakes and regrets. Let her know that staying stuck in a place of regret only hurts the present and future time she has with her children. Encourage her with the Apostle Paul's words, "But I focus on one thing: Forgetting the past and looking forward to what lies ahead" (Philippians 3:13).

Group Tips

+ Avoid minimizing and trivializing.

Not all women experience the same depth of empty-nest syndrome—or maybe there are some women in your ministry whose kids haven't left home yet. Make sure your group is supportive, even when some (or all) members cannot relate with the empty-nest mom's struggles. Help her validate all of the emotions she experiences.

+ Appreciate differences.

Creating a culture in which your group appreciates differences in each other is an important piece of fellowship, community, and growth. Set a tone in which group members embrace each other's different stages, phases, and places of life and are able to learn from one another. Maybe the empty-nest mom can give tips to the pre-empty-nest moms about what to expect in this season of life.

+ Avoid comparing.

Women have a propensity to compare marriages, husbands, emotional health, finances, bodies, and so on. This can be very destructive—especially if a struggling empty nester sees that other women don't seem as devastated as she is. Help your group steer clear of comparisons.

What Not to Say

+ "Don't you worry about your kids?"

Yes, if you're a mom, you worry about your kids. We don't need a reminder of the myriad disasters and problems our kids may be encountering. The same goes for recounting the horrors that are happening on a campus or town similar to the one where the child is.

+ "What are you going to do with all of your time?"

When kids leave home, there's less to do, but it doesn't make one less of a person, which this can imply. It can also underscore the loneliness they're feeling. Ask about the new things they're able to do instead.

+ "Now you can have time for yourself."

Even though this may be true, it is not a comforting statement for a woman grieving over her children leaving home.

+ "Just call your son every day."

Encouraging an empty-nest mom to be overbearing and over-involved in the life of a child who has gone off to college or gotten married can be bad advice. Help your friend establish new healthy boundaries with her child.

+ "I felt such freedom when they all moved out. Try and look at it that way."

This kind of comment may be meant to encourage but actually it can do just the opposite. It can compound the empty-nest mom's feeling of sadness and make her feel worse about herself. Instead, point out the positive things you've experienced since your child left home.

What to Say

+ "Let's get some stuff and make care packages."
We all love doing things for our kids. Holidays and semester exams are good excuses to send love in a tangible way. If everyone provides one or two things for all of the kids, there'll be a good assortment of fun stuff to send. You'll build relationships with friends, too.

+ "Let's surprise the singles group."
The people in the young singles group at church (or students at a nearby college) may be away from their families, too. Surprise them with treats, valentines, or a home-cooked meal. Don't you want someone to be doing the same for your kids?

+ "Having kids sure helps us understand God's love for us."
God lets us make choices, try new things, go our own way. When we do the same with our kids, we begin to sense, in a small way, how God might feel about us and our choices.

+ "I'll call you tomorrow."
If she's lonely, give her a call regularly. Listen and look for ways to help her find meaningful things to do. Find reasons to laugh, exercise, and volunteer. She has lots to offer to this world and you can help her find it.

+ "Do you want to play tennis? go on a walk? go to the art museum?"
Asking the empty-nest mom to join you for an activity can be very therapeutic. It will probably offer a welcomed distraction and give her an opportunity to enjoy herself.

+ "What kind of things are you thinking about doing now that you have more time?"

It can be helpful to gently ask and discuss the empty-nest mom's thoughts about career, ministry, hobbies, and travel. Helping her see this phase of life as an opportunity to grow in her relationship with God can bring hope.

SCRIPTURE HELP

+ **Proverbs 17:6**
+ **Proverbs 31:10-31**
+ **Ecclesiastes 3:1-14**
+ **Matthew 6:25-34**
+ **Luke 8:1-15**

+ **1 Corinthians 13**
+ **Ephesians 6:10-18**
+ **1 Thessalonians 5:16-18**
+ **James 5:13-16**

ADDITIONAL RESOURCES

+ Books

Empty Nest...Full Heart: The Journey from Home to College. Andrea Van Steenhouse. Denver, CO: Simpler Life Press, 2002.

When You're Facing the Empty Nest: Avoiding Midlife Meltdown When Your Child Leaves Home. Mary Ann Froehlich. Minneapolis, MN Bethany House, 2005.

She's Leaving Home: Letting Go as Daughter Goes to College, Connie Jones. Kansas City, MO: Andrews McMeel Publishing, 2002.

+ Online Resources

www.emptynestmoms.com
www.emptynestsupport.com

WHEN TO REFER

✚ When a woman seems to be experiencing depression

If an empty-nest mom experiences changes in her sleeping patterns, weight changes, inability to concentrate, has weeping spells, or loses interest in things she used to enjoy, she might benefit from seeing a professional counselor.

✚ Refer empty-nest women having serious marriage struggles

If an empty-nest woman finds herself having ongoing difficulty in her marriage, refer her to a marriage counselor.

✚ Refer empty-nest women with multiple stressors

If an empty-nest woman has several different stressors going on in her life at the same time (aging parents, health problems, work-related pressures, and so on), you may want to refer her to a counselor who can help her sift through and manage the different stress-causing issues.

IMPORTANT FACTS

ABOUT EMPTY-NEST SYNDROME

✚ The number of "boomerang kids" is increasing—nearly one in three unmarried adults now lives with a parent.

✚ After retirement, 43 percent of baby boomers still plan to work, while 44 percent are undecided.

CHAPTER SEVEN

Infidelity/Adultery

Supporting Your Friend Through an Affair

with counseling insights from **PAUL FRIESEN, PH.D.**
+ ministry tips from **LINDA CRAWFORD**

November 2003

God has perfect timing. Ron and I had wanted to attend a couples retreat for a very long time. So we went, just the two of us. It was the first time in about six years we had had this kind of getaway. I was so excited to be there and focus on my marriage, and felt so close to God. We prayed a lot and talked, and I was on a high.

The session right before we broke for lunch was on resolving conflict and forgiveness. Then Ron and I set off for lunch. We grabbed a sandwich and pulled into a parking area to eat and visit a bit. It was then that he turned to me with this look on his face and said that he needed to make sure that I understood what he had done. I didn't know what he was talking about. My husband of 10 years then told me that throughout our marriage he had had several affairs, and that he had lied to me the whole time.

I couldn't breathe. I sat there in silence and literally could not believe what I had just heard. Ron was in a career where it made it easy for him to hide, with no close friendships to hold him accountable and a wife who always gave him the benefit of the doubt. He told me he'd had a problem for as long as he could remember and had always tried to deal with it himself. He had never turned that part of his life over to God and had in many ways been leading two lives. He said he had now given his life completely to God and that the first thing God wanted him to do was to tell me.

I had so many thoughts and questions swimming around in my head, but what I had learned at the conference was quite clear. I felt God take control. I had prayed to him just before we left for lunch and asked him to take control of my life in all areas. My heart hurt so badly, but I had this incredible peace.

The first couple of days after the affairs were revealed, I would wake up in the middle of the night and panic about anyone going through this same hurt who didn't know Jesus. It was so clear to me that I had found out everything just at the right time. If Ron had told this to me before the conference weekend, the outcome would have been disastrous, and I would have let it destroy me.

November 2004

I feel like I am dangling from a rope in a dark hole. I feel so isolated and desperate, and yet I know who is holding my rope. I do have hope. I believe God wholeheartedly, and I know he will carry me through all of this.

It is very frustrating to be a cheerleader type of a person and feel so unenthusiastic. I'm tired of being sad and feeling like everywhere I go I have a dark rain cloud overhead, just following me. I don't like having that sinking feeling every time someone asks me how I'm doing, especially if they know nothing about my life for the past year.

It was so hard to find out that Ron has a son, especially when I always wanted a son. My life feels so surreal sometimes. I was gaining such strength, but the past week I've felt broken, like I am literally in pieces. God, please give me strength once again, heal my heart, and help me to accept the hand I've been dealt and play it properly. Please bless our two little girls that lie asleep across the hall. They are so precious and are truly great blessings you have given me.

I know you've got big plans for my life, and I feel you working deep in my soul. It just hurts so bad at times. I can't handle it all, and I know you don't want me to, so here it is. I give it up.

April 2005

I feel there are some definite role-expectations issues that need to be addressed. We've tried all this time to remain in a marriage relationship while dealing with some very big issues. I've tried stepping forward instead of stepping back, but what is happening is an unhealthy cycle that I don't want anymore. It doesn't feel right. For me, there is love and attraction, but I don't want to build my future on that alone. Proceeding with life like nothing has happened and feeling like I have to assume my wifely role while having so many underlying feelings makes me feel like I'm a bad wife. We are broken, working on things, hurting, learning, searching, but not normal. To everyone looking in, things appear relatively appropriate—but the feelings don't match. This isn't right. It's not healthy. It's screaming inside at me. I'm going to listen. I want God's marriage. I will fight for it with everything that I am.

June 2005

How do I feel? Very conflicted. I've loved Ron for so long and so much that I can't hate him, and he's betrayed and hurt me so deeply that I can't wholeheartedly love him. So I go day by day with this uncomfortable feeling of playing the role of wife but not having the emotions that should go along with it. I can't simply erase all that's been said and done and pretend that they didn't take a toll. They have; they've taken a huge toll.

I want peace and joy and for things to just be simpler. God hates divorce, but he hates adultery even more—it's the only biblical grounds for divorce. So does God feel that this is what is best? Or is it optional? What in my case? I want more than anything in this whole world for my girls to have a family that consists of their mother and father. They deserve to witness a deeply loving relationship, one that will still have ups and downs, but that has God in the center. Will God have that happen here? Will he restore behaviors and feelings and relationships? I am desperately hanging in there to find out.

February 2006

I remember sitting at the first few home group meetings and listening to what others were saying. As hard as it was, I contacted a sweet, kind-hearted woman from our home group and another woman who was a previous pastor's wife and reached out. They have been my hands of God. The person I confided in from our group is someone who walks with the Lord, and the way she spoke of her relationship with God was something I longed for. I now have it.

My husband has sought professional counsel and has reached out to some good Christian men to hold him accountable. We pray out loud together daily, as strongly urged at the conference, and it's making a huge difference. When I look at my Ron, the darkness and anger that was there before is gone, and I pray it never returns. We have a long road ahead of us and a lot to deal with.

WHEN TO REFER

Most women who have experienced an affair in their marriage can benefit from some individual counseling to help them sort out their feelings and recreate their identity in their marriages. Also be on the lookout for symptoms of depression and thoughts of suicide—then refer immediately.

Couples counseling might also be in order, especially for couples who are making the difficult decision about whether or not to continue their marriage.

SCRIPTURE HELP

+ **Psalm 31:24**
+ **Psalm 46:1**
+ **Psalm 68:19**
+ **Psalm 119:49-50**
+ **Proverbs 3:5-6**

+ **Isaiah 41:10**
+ **Isaiah 43:2-3**
+ **Romans 5:1-5**
+ **Philippians 4:13**
+ **2 Thessalonians 2:16-17**
+ **2 Thessalonians 3:16**

Care and Counseling Tips

THE BASICS

When a husband chooses to engage in an emotional or sexual relationship outside of his marriage, it is among the most devastating news his wife can receive. The man who committed to stand with her and face any trial that comes her way in life is now intentionally causing her the deepest pain imaginable. She begins to question who she is: Is she no longer enough for him? What has she done or not done that would cause her husband to choose another over her? What will she need to do to win him back? Should she try to resolve things or just leave him?

Whether the affair was physical or emotional, trust is broken and self-doubt creeps into the marriage relationship. When women experience this painful discovery, they may feel intense emotions. Women often feel guilt, shame, grief, and anger—or a mixture of all of these and more. More than ever before, she now needs the support of the women in your ministry to help her.

Care Tips

The good news is that social support received by others can minimize the long-term damage of an affair on the heart and soul of a woman and her family. Caring for your friend's practical needs in a time of crisis is an important expression of Christ's love and will solidify your commitment to walk with the person through the difficult experience. The following suggestions focus on how you can help with the woman's immediate needs:

✚ Listen nonjudgmentally.

If your friend has just discovered that her husband is engaging in an affair, she probably has many emotions—anger, fear, grief, questioning. She may be wondering what the future of her marriage will be and what her role as a wife should look like. Resist the urge to offer solutions at this point. Listen to her concerns and pray with her about her fears.

✚ Encourage her to get help quickly.

Tell your friend, "I may not be the person to counsel you through this, but you need to get help immediately." Giving the situation time to work itself out only allows it to develop. Instead, connect your friend or the couple with a Christian counselor.

Also help your friend set firm limits with her husband. For example, instead of allowing him endless weeks to make decisions that affect their marriage, she should tell him he has 24 hours to choose between her or his mistress. This firm boundary will help the couple determine the course of their future relationship.

✚ Don't attempt to assess each person's degree of responsibility.

Many women feel guilty about not spending enough time with their husbands, not meeting their needs, or not being available to them. Help your friend understand that her husband is solely responsible for his choices and needs to be accountable for his sin. Though this doesn't mean she can't be involved in improving the marriage, she shouldn't blame herself for the affair.

✛ Insist that her husband be tested for sexually transmitted diseases.

Husbands will often say that they only had "protected sex" or never actually had intercourse. For your friend's safety, he should be tested for STDs. Have her ask the doctor how long he should refrain from sexual activity while waiting for the results.

✛ Encourage your friend to focus on her relationship with the Lord.

Though God might feel very far away in such devastating circumstances, remind your friend that this is a time to rely on him most. She might find this especially difficult because her trust in her husband has been shattered. Commit to praying for and with her.

IMPORTANT FACTS

ABOUT ADULTERY

✛ One of the top spots that married individuals meet affair partners is at the workplace.

✛ Although definitive numbers are hard to come by, most estimates report that one-third of men and one-quarter of women admit to at least one extramarital sexual act.

✛ Emotional infidelity, in which a spouse engages in an intimate (though not sexual) friendship with the opposite sex, occurs at a much higher rate, probably over 50 percent.

Counseling Tips

✚ Believe that God is able to reconcile their relationship.

An affair is devastating at best, but does not need to be a marriage-ending event. God is able to take that which Satan meant for evil and use it for good when couples respond to him and allow him to bring healing to their relationship. God is able to show his incredible power in restoring that which was dead back to life.

✚ Create an atmosphere of honesty in the family.

After the couple has had an opportunity to discuss their relationship together and with a Christian counselor, they may question how much information to give their children. This depends on the ages and maturity of their kids, but in general, the couple should be honest about the situation. Many couples make the mistake of covering up or lying about the affair to their children, which leads to more broken trust. Instead, as the person responsible for the affair, the husband should be the one to inform them in an age-appropriate manner about what happened.

✚ Decide who should know.

Couples often wonder whom they should tell about the infidelity. Their first instinct may be to cover up what happened. Though it's difficult to share such painful information, telling the truth is freeing for the couple and allows others to surround them with support.

The couple should consult with their Christian counselor to help them decide who to tell. Some counselors believe that the people who should be included in the circle of disclosure should equal the people in the couple's sphere of influence. For example, if a senior pastor had the affair, he should consider disclosing the affair to the entire congregation; a small group leader should inform the members of the small group; a church member should tell his family. Being truthful about the situation eliminates the possibility of breeding rumors and creating distortions.

+ Encourage your friend to ask questions.

Sometimes men say, "I was sexually inappropriate with someone else, but it would hurt you more if I told you the details." Is that true? Many counselors believe that it's not healthy to withhold information in this situation. The wife should be given the opportunity, in a safe setting such as a counseling appointment, to ask as many questions as she needs to. Her husband then has the responsibility of fully answering her questions truthfully. Unanswered questions will only continue to haunt the couple. It's up to the couple and their counselor, through prayer, to decide how to handle the situation.

ADDITIONAL RESOURCES

+ Books

Restoring the Fallen: A Team Approach to Caring, Confronting, and Reconciling. Sandy Wilson, Paul Friesen, Virginia Friesen, Larry Paulson, and Nancy Paulson. Downers Grove, IL: InterVarsity Press, 1997.

Surviving an Affair. Willard F. Harley Jr. and Jennifer Harley Chalmers. Grand Rapids, MI: Revell, 1998.

I Don't Love You Anymore: What to Do When He Says. David Clarke. Nashville, TN: Thomas Nelson, 2002.

Separated and Waiting. Jan Northington. Wake Forest, NC: Church Initiative, 1994.

+ Online Resources

www.growthtrac.com (Growthtrac)
www.family.org (Focus on the Family)
www.churchinitiative.org

Group Tips

✚ Be a listening ear.
This news is devastating. Let her tell her story. Be slow to hop in with something like "I know just how you feel…"

✚ Be tight-lipped.
Don't engage in gossip with others in your ministry. Allow your friend the dignity of sharing her situation with those she trusts.

✚ Do something.
The realization of a cheating spouse is a life-altering event. Your friend may be in shock and feel overwhelmed by decisions she must make. Don't just ask, "What can I do?"—find a practical way to help out. Bring food, baby-sit her kids, clean her house. Do something that will lighten her load.

✚ Pair with a mentor couple.
Find a couple in your church who would be willing to mentor your friend and her husband. It could be a couple who has experienced an affair, but it doesn't have to be. Have them meet as a foursome, and also separately as husbands and wives. This mentor relationship can be a safe place to explore the possibilities for the future of the marriage.

What Not to Say

✦ "You have biblical grounds for divorce."

As a friend, you should never say this to another woman. If she is a Christian, she already knows this. She will be praying and seeking God for his direction for her marriage. What she really needs is not your analysis of the situation or your judgment of right/wrong, but your support of her prayers. If she has questions she needs biblical guidance on, direct her to a pastor or qualified Christian counselor to help her sort things out. Pray for God's will for her life, not yours.

✦ "You'll be better off without him."

Ouch. You have just deeply insulted your friend. She has loved this man and entered into a covenant of marriage with him. Words like these devalue the relationship as well as insensitively suggest that she should simply discard him like trash and get on with life. Honor your friend and God by avoiding negative talk about her husband. Persevere with her in the healing process she believes God has for her—for as long as it takes.

✦ "I know what you must be feeling."

Women who have been hurt by adultery can feel very isolated and alone; however, now is not the time to express understanding by sharing *your* story. Most women have been wounded by a failed relationship at some point in their lives, but every experience is very personal and unique. Don't be surprised if your friend reacts with stony silence if you attempt to comfort her in this way. She doesn't need her story compared to yours. She needs you to listen to how *she* feels, not how you feel.

✦ "What did he see in her that you don't have?"

Was she better looking, was she more athletic, was she more available sexually, was she more fun, or did she affirm him more than the wife did? Does he love his mistress more than his wife?

Most women try to logically make sense out of why he did what he did. Adultery is not a logical issue. It is a sinful choice to covet that which you don't have and act sinfully to obtain it. This issue is not is she prettier, wittier, more charming, and so on. Once we are married, we are not allowed to look around to see if we want to upgrade.

+ "He didn't have sex with her, so it wasn't an affair."

Don't minimize the offense. When someone confides in a person other than his or her spouse, an emotional bond is created. Emotional affairs can be equally as, if not more, devastating as physical ones. This includes online relationships as well as physical ones.

Additionally, pornography lures many men into addictions that cause their spouses much the same pain as actual affairs. In this case, the husband needs to follow the same steps of confession, repentance, and restitution as he would after a physical affair. He may also need addiction counseling.

What to Say

+ "I'm behind you."

Your friend has lost a solid foundation in her life, and she may feel like she is now sinking in quicksand. She needs people in her life to help her keep her head above the sand. People she can depend on—who will do what they say, and say what they will do. Be one of those who will listen, support, and encourage her through the tears and the struggle for direction and healing. Hold her up and build her up as she learns to walk forward again to solid ground.

+ "Let me help with the kids."

Everyone needs a break from responsibilities in stressful times, and now is one of the best times to offer practical help. Your friend needs time away to pray, rest, and find strength for the journey. If she has children, offer to watch the kids so she can go to a funny movie, have coffee with a friend, or enjoy a relaxing massage. Invite her for weekly walks in the park for fresh air and exercise. Be available for those tasks that are overwhelming to her—paying the bills, running the kids to appointments, or picking up the dry cleaning. These little actions are the large acts of love she needs right now.

✛ "How can I pray for you?"

Be sensitive to the timing and type of prayer support you offer your friend right now. She may feel embarrassed and ashamed to have people know about her situation. She may not be comfortable sharing details or her specific prayer needs, but she desperately needs your prayers. Ask if she has a favorite Scripture or find an uplifting one, and then commit to praying it for her daily. You may think, "It's the least I can do," but don't diminish the importance of your support role in prayer. She needs every friend who will take the time to lift her up in prayer—it's the least and the most you can do!

✛ "We live in a broken world, and that affects everything —even love."

It can be a meaningful experience to acknowledge that the brokenness, sinfulness, and grief we experience are so far from God's ideal for us. Some women find it easy to turn to God in the midst of suffering. For others, it's a difficult task to trust in God's goodness. Life on this earth is often unfair, and many times it can feel like there is no justice in the aftermath of an affair. Longing together for our eternal life with Christ can be a helpful reminder of the new heaven and earth in store for Christians.

WHEN WOMEN CHEAT

A woman in your ministry approaches you and confesses she is having an affair. She asks what you think she should do. What should you say?

Some people think it's better not to confess to their spouse, in order to avoid causing them pain. However, this is not the best advice to give your friend—eventually the truth will come out. She and her husband can only experience intimacy in their marriage to the degree that they have honesty.

Encourage your friend to find a time to admit to her husband what she has done. Help her create a safe environment for this, such as a counseling session, or offer to watch her kids so they can have some private discussion time together.

If your friend struggles with following through on this, it's not your place to inform her husband yourself. You can continue to support your friend and encourage her to be honest, but the decision to tell her husband should be hers.

CHAPTER EIGHT

Infertility
Walking With Women Through
the Emotional Roller Coaster

with counseling insights from **MAGGIE H. ROBBINS, MA**
+ ministry tips from **CHRISTINA SCHOFIELD
& AMBER VAN SCHOONEVELD**

Stacey is my best friend from college. Back then, we would stay up half the night with a bag of Oreos talking about boys and wondering what our lives would be like. We both wanted the usual stuff—a husband who was super-hot with the sensitivities of Oprah, a cozy home with room for lots of shoes, and gorgeous blonde children playing quietly in a flowered meadow. Is it any wonder things didn't go quite as planned?

Most of us gals have been preparing for our families since we were small. I meticulously groomed my dolls, cutting their hair military style, decorating them with markers, hurling them from the bed into the dirty clothes hamper over and over (what can I say? I liked basketball, too). To find out after years of dreaming that having a baby just isn't possible is downright devastating.

This is just where Stacey found herself a few years ago.

Emergency Response Handbook: *How long have you been trying to conceive?*

Stacey: It's been three years since we've been trying. We tried for about one year before the doctor decided to have us start getting tested. After testing my husband, they found there was nothing wrong with him.

Then they tested me and couldn't find anything wrong with me either. We decided to try intrauterine insemination (IUI).

I remember the nurses saying I would be so easy to get pregnant because there didn't seem to be anything wrong with me. They said it was a closed case; it would work.

ERH: *How did that make you feel?*

Stacey: It gave me such hope. I thought for sure it was going to work. But when it didn't work, that made it even harder. To get your hopes up so high and then have it not work out was really hard.

ERH: *Where did you go from there?*

Stacey: We went through three different rounds of IUI. At the same time, we were doing everything else we could, tracking my ovulation, doing all the little things people tell you will help.

It was an emotional roller coaster. I would be in the doctor's office several times a week, and I would start getting my hopes up. But I still never got pregnant.

ERH: *What's one of the hardest parts of your struggle?*

Stacey: Constantly getting asked about it. People are always asking me when I'm going to start having kids or why I haven't yet. They tell me how wonderful it is and that I really ought to have kids. They have no idea the emotional storm I'm already going through at the time and how much those words hurt.

ERH: *What else?*

Stacey: The people who do know about my struggle can make it hard, too. People are always trying to give you assurances. They say, "Oh, it'll work; it'll happen." But it's three years later, and it still hasn't. They don't know if it'll happen, and I wish they wouldn't say it. People also try to tell you a lot of stories of friends who struggled for years to get pregnant, then adopted and got pregnant right away. Or someone who just did this and got pregnant, or did that and got pregnant. When you're trying to conceive, you're constantly thinking about it, about what you could be doing or should be doing. And it's hard to have that advice always coming, because it doesn't always work.

ERH: *If your friend knows you're trying to conceive, do you want her to ask you about how it's going?*

Stacey: It depends on the person. If you're really close to the person, then yes, they can ask. But it gets hard when too many people keep asking you if you've gotten pregnant; sometimes you just don't want to think about it. It's also hard when people show excitement, asking, "Has it worked?!" And then you have to say no.

ERH: *What would you want a friend to do for you?*

Stacey: I want my friends to just say that they know I'm trying and they know it's hard, but that they'll listen to me if I need to talk. I don't want any cliché statements, just support.

The thing that helps the most is talking to someone else who has gone through the same thing. I have a friend who is also trying to have a child, and she understands how I'm feeling. A lot of people don't talk about this struggle—it's unspoken. There's this stigma that you're failing or there's something wrong with you. So you don't always know who else is struggling with infertility.

ERH: *How has your family helped you in this?*

Stacey: My family has been really helpful. They've been accepting of me and supportive. They ask me what they can do to help. They don't assume anything, and they don't try to push their views on me about what I should do or why it's not working. I know women who can't conceive whose mothers or mothers-in-law get really upset with them because they want grandchildren. My family hasn't put that pressure on me, which is really helpful.

It's great to have friends and family who support you whether or not you ever have a child and who keep loving you no matter what.

Care and Counseling Tips

THE BASICS

Infertility is the inability to conceive a child after at least one year of trying. The psychological implications can be extreme and far-reaching. The intense biological drive to have children coupled with societal, familial, and internal pressure can cause serious emotional pain that can interfere with all aspects of a woman's life. Our culture has historically placed a high status on motherhood. A woman's inability to join that sacred and powerful club can make her feel alone in her grief. When facing infertility, the woman has to accept the challenge of redefining her identity. With support, guidance, and counseling, a woman can resolve her feelings of loss and continue to have a meaningful and productive life.

✛ Emotional Impact

When a woman finds out she is infertile, she will most likely progress through several steps on her path toward acceptance. She will begin with *surprise*, followed by *denial*, then *anger*—at herself, her situation, her husband, couples who have children, and even God. She may experience *isolation*, feeling like no one understands, *guilt* over such powerful negative emotions, *grief* over her loss, and hopefully *acceptance*. She won't necessarily move through the steps in this particular order, and she may seem to improve, only to regress in response to a new infertility crisis or stressful time period. Depression is likely in a woman who is facing infertility. Feelings of powerlessness, helplessness, and a lack of hope for the future are probable emotions.

✛ Relational Impact

Relational problems are likely with many important people in her life. Marital problems often arise, and can result in blame, financial strain, and a disagreement over how to proceed with fertility treatment and when to stop trying. Infertility poses a great threat to a marriage. The grief can be intense, putting up walls between the couple. The woman may feel like other important people in her life do not understand what she is going through, further isolating her from the support she will desperately need to get through her grief.

WHEN TO REFER

+ Suicidal thoughts
If the woman has mentioned harming herself or not having a reason to live, make sure she is safe and refer her to a licensed counselor immediately.

+ Lingering depression
Depression is a normal reaction to a crisis, but if it seems to last a long time or impacts the woman's daily functioning, she may need professional help.

+ Conflicted marriage
This will be a real test of the couple's marriage. Couples counseling may be necessary to maintain the health of the relationship.

Care Tips

If you discover that a woman in your ministry is dealing with infertility, support her in the following ways:

✛ Make yourself available to talk, but don't force the issue.

Allowing the woman the chance to talk without putting any pressure on her will let her know you care. You can also empower her to decide when to begin discussing her loss.

✛ Suggest a support group.

Support from others who have similar struggles is invaluable. There are many types of support groups available these days. They can be easily located through the national Web sites (see Additional Resources box on page 111), fertility doctors, or at the hospital.

✛ Encourage self-care.

Offer to schedule a massage or a manicure for your friend. Go for a walk or a bike ride together, or help her make time to take a bath or read a good book. Self-care is critical in times of stress but may be the last thing she would think of.

✛ Offer specific help.

Instead of a general offer to help out, suggest specific things you can help with. Ask if you could bring dinner over one night or drive her to a doctor's appointment. She will be more likely to accept help if you suggest some practical things you can do.

✛ Don't forget about her husband.

He will also be grieving and in shock, and it will be hard for them to take care of each other at this point. They will both need outside support.

Connect your friend's husband with other Christian men that he can lean on during this stressful time. Having some "guy time" away from the tension can help him support his wife more when they are together.

+ Provide a referral to a fertility specialist and an adoption agency.

When the couple is ready, they may want to begin exploring their options, but may not have the energy to seek out specialists. Wait until they approach you before offering this type of information.

SCRIPTURE HELP

+ 1 Samuel 1:9–2:11
+ Job 30
+ Psalm 5:2-3
+ Psalm 55:22
+ Psalm 121

+ Psalm 139:1-5, 14-16
+ Psalm 147:3-5
+ Colossians 4:2
+ James 1:17-18
+ 1 Peter 5:7

Counseling Tips

By helping your friend deal with powerful emotions about her loss, you can help her learn to form a new identity and prepare for treatment.

+ Help her identify her strengths.
In hard times it is easy to forget that she has strengths. The woman in your ministry may need help to remember what she does well. Help her recognize how her strengths have worked in the past and encourage her to apply those lessons to her current situation. Encourage her to make a list of her strengths and post it where she can see it regularly.

+ Suggest counseling.
Experiencing infertility takes a toll on a marriage. Encourage your friend and her husband to turn toward each other during this difficult time, instead of allowing the stress and grief to separate them. A third party can aid in good communication and help clear up disagreements and misunderstandings.

+ Explore feelings of powerlessness and helplessness.
Your friend may not know how to handle feeling a loss of control. Help her explore this new terrain, while empowering her to make healthy decisions for herself. Together you can identify the areas of her life where she does have power to make decisions.

+ Be aware of an increase of acting-out behaviors.
An increase in harmful behaviors is likely after a trauma. Gently point out problem behaviors such as excessive drinking, drug use, eating disorders, and extramarital affairs that may jeopardize her ability to resolve her feelings about her infertility.

Group Tips

+ Decrease Isolation.

Help your friend remember the beautiful parts of life by visiting a museum, planting a garden, taking a hike, or watching a sunset. She will need people around her more than usual—don't wait for her to ask for support.

+ Be hopeful for her.

Groups have the power to shift the energy of a situation. If the woman is having trouble feeling hopeful, feel it for her, and share your continued hope with her on a regular basis. Eventually she might just be persuaded to join in on the good feelings.

+ Organize an informational group on fertility options.

Being informed is a good step toward feeling empowerment. This will allow the woman to make good decisions about her future. If possible, suggest that she help organize the event. Acting on her own behalf can help her feel a sense of empowerment that will move her in the right direction.

+ Be practical.

Go with your friend to doctor's appointments, in case she needs someone to help her ask questions or to cry with. If your friend is busy with tests and appointments or is simply overwhelmed with emotions, arrange meals to be made for however long she needs them. Give your friend a care basket to let her know that she's special and you care for her—including items to help her unwind and relax, such as bubble bath, tea, and foot scrubs. These practical little ideas can make a big difference.

+ Form a support group.

Often, women who have experienced infertility want to talk to women who have had the same experience. But the stigma of infertility and the personal nature of the subject often isolates women. Create a safe place in your ministry for women to come and support one another as they discuss their experiences.

IMPORTANT FACTS

ABOUT INFERTILITY

✚ Approximately 10 percent of American couples, six million couples, are affected by infertility.

✚ At least 25 percent of couples facing infertility have more than one factor causing infertility.

✚ Problems with ovulation account for 25 percent of infertility.

✚ Factors affecting the fallopian tubes and lining of the pelvis and abdomen account for 35 percent of infertility.

✚ In approximately 40 percent of couples, the male is either the contributing or sole cause of infertility.

What Not to Say

+ "So when are you going to start having kids?"

You never know what the person you're asking this of has been going through. She may have been silently struggling for years to conceive or had miscarriages, and, if she's a certain age, she's probably heard this question way too many times. It's often a painful and unwanted reminder.

+ "Don't let it get you down."

Of course infertility will get a person "down." This statement dismisses the problem as insignificant rather than offering support or encouragement. Instead, tell your friend that you can't understand how hard it must be, but that you love her and want to support her.

+ "You're still young; it'll happen."

Don't make promises—you don't know what God has for that person, and it may not be motherhood. If a woman repeatedly hears that "of course it's going to happen," it will be that much more crushing if it does not. Only God knows whether or not this couple will ever be able to conceive.

+ "You can always adopt."

Pretty sure your friend has already thought of this. A statement like this can belittle the sense of pain and loss they are dealing with. Not to mention, adoption is a really personal decision people should make in their own time.

+ "Go on a second honeymoon; just try and relax."

This implies that the woman has control over her infertility. Many women are told that if they'd just stop stressing out and relax, they'd conceive. Besides that, it simply might not be true—your friend might be infertile, not just stressed. Don't assure her it will happen if she just adjusts her attitude.

What to Say

✛ "What can I do to help you?"
It's OK not to know what to say or do. Most likely, your friend will just want to know that you care and that you want to help her in whatever way she needs.

✛ "I'm so sorry for your loss."
Your friend will be going through the grieving process. Allow her to feel sad and mourn, and mourn with her. Keep it simple; share your feelings with her. Try to remain open with how you are feeling. This will show her it is all right for her to do the same.

✛ "God really does love you."
Your friend might feel invisible to God. "Why doesn't he hear my prayers?" Take her to Psalm 139—God knows her through and through and thinks of her constantly. There is no end to his love for her, even if she feels forgotten.

✛ "You are special. Period."
A woman who isn't able to have children feels displaced. "What is my purpose in life?" Reassure her that she is completely special because God made her. She is valuable just because of who she is, regardless of the direction her life takes.

✛ "You are not alone."
Grief is its own world. Introduce your friend to someone in a similar situation who can truly empathize with what she is going through. (Try an online Christian forum, like ShilohGarden). Be sure she knows you are there for her and you won't get tired of listening if she needs to talk.

✦ "You should do what is best for you and your husband."

Every situation is different, and there is no one "right" course of action. Whatever the couple decides—to pursue treatment, to stop trying to conceive, to adopt—support them as they follow God's will for their lives.

ADDITIONAL RESOURCES

✦ Books

Crisis Intervention: Theory and Methodology. Donna C. Aguilera. St. Louis, MO: Mosby Press, 1998.

Counseling Depressed Women. Susan J. Dunlap. Louisville, KY: Westminster John Knox Press, 1998.

Inconceivable Conceptions: Psychological Aspects of Infertility and Reproductive Technology. Jane Haynes and Juliet Miller, Eds. Hove, England: Brunner-Routledge, 2003.

Inconceivable: Finding Peace in the Midst of Infertility. Shannon Woodward. Colorado Springs, CO: Cook Communications Ministries, 2006.

✦ Online Resources

www.resolve.org (The National Infertility Association)
www.theafa.org (The American Fertility Association)
www.inciid.org (InterNational Council on Infertility Information Dissemination, Inc.)

CHAPTER NINE

Menopause
Helping Women Adjust
to Physical Changes

with counseling insights from **LAURA GREINER, PH.D.**
+ ministry tips from **HEATHER DUNN**

I don't remember exactly when the hot flashes started. They were a surprise, and I wasn't sure whether to make fun of them or just ignore them. Sometimes they happened at work, mostly they happened overnight. I'd wake up and throw off the covers—even in the winter. I'd lay there dripping sweat. I was grateful that they mostly happened at home.

I'd always had a predictable monthly period, so when I had one that started early on our vacation, I was surprised. I became alarmed when it lasted for four weeks. The doctor said it was the beginning of an unpredictable time. Boy, was she right. After that, I never really knew when to expect one. Sometimes I could skip several months, sometimes I'd only have a week in between. Sometimes they'd be unbelievably heavy, other times they'd be almost nothing. Sometimes they'd start slowly, other times they'd start with a gush. I could never predict. I kept a change of clothes in the car and extra supplies in my purse.

I had headaches, too. They seemed to be tied to my cycle, but since that wasn't predictable, neither were my headaches. Occasionally they were awful; mostly they were a nuisance.

I gained some weight. Before, I could maintain a fairly normal weight by eating sensible portions and not overdoing the desserts. That wasn't working now. I didn't feel nearly as attractive as I used to. I was never a beauty queen and tried to brush it off as being too worldly to be concerned about my outward appearance. But I did try to look nice and professional. Now my clothes were tight.

My hair, though it had been showing little streaks of grey, now turned completely so. I'd been coloring it for years to cover up the streaks, but I could see the changes just before I added color every few months. The color didn't work the same, either. And it wasn't just the hair on my head that changed. Even my eyebrows turned so you could hardly see them unless I drew in the lines.

How many blows can there be to one's ego? Well, there were more. I found myself being forgetful. I'd forget names of friends who were standing right in front of me. I'd forget where I put my glasses, which were now bifocals. I worried about my forgetfulness, thinking I would surely be diagnosed with a serious illness. I began paying attention to all of my aches and pains and wondering if this downhill slide would only escalate and thinking that my end was surely near.

I was cranky with my husband. He couldn't win no matter what. I wanted him to notice me, but not my changes. If he brushed over them, however, I would be irritated. If he admitted that my appearance had changed, that was unacceptable, too. If he made light of things, he wasn't being sensitive. If he took them seriously, he wasn't being sensitive, either. If he wanted to spend time with me, I wanted to be alone. If he left me alone, I wanted him to spend time with me. Like I said, he couldn't win. I could look at the situation and realize that I wasn't being rational or fair. That just made me crankier!

So this is menopause, I thought. How dandy! I was discouraged about my appearance, irritated about the way I treated my husband, and worried about what my body might do next. My family was never very good about talking about personal things, so this had never been discussed. My mom, with whom I had felt closest to, had died of cancer, so my best confidante was no longer around anyway. We'd moved recently, so my old friends didn't live close by. The move had monopolized my time, so I hadn't stayed in touch very well. Many of my friends were younger anyway, so I knew they wouldn't be interested. I wasn't crazy about discussing it with my husband, either. So, mostly I brooded and felt sorry for myself.

If I could go back and do one thing differently, I would talk more with others. Had I talked more with doctors, I'd have felt better about what was happening. They would have reassured me and helped me with my questions and issues. Had I talked with friends, I'd have found that I was pretty normal. I'd have found that the season passes, and there is normalcy on the other side. I'd have found some support and deepened some relationships. I'd have done less worrying and more laughing. Had I talked more with my husband, I'd have found more support, too. Well, maybe. It wasn't really his lack of support but my unwillingness to accept it.

Now that I'm pretty much through it, I look back and chuckle. I was really cranky. I was pretty selfish. I was vain, too. Mostly, I was selfish. It was all about me. I realized that I had to come to terms with who I was and how I was defining myself. Am I an old woman? Am I no longer attractive to my husband? Am I past my prime?

Guess what I figured out! I'm still a kid in God's eyes. I'm God's kid, no matter what my age or physical condition happens to be. God gave me a body to inhabit and enjoy. When I define myself in God's terms instead of my own, it's a whole different perspective. And, it's not just that "God looks at the inside while the world looks at the outside" sort of thing.

I let my hair become its natural color. I get lots of compliments on its beauty. I like the grey. I exercise regularly and feel much better. I actually feel younger. I skip when I'm happy and giggle at my wrinkles (OK, my wiggles, too, which I have plenty of). I prefer to think of the lines at the edges of my eyes as grin marks, because they show up extra when I smile. My husband still puts up with me, just like I put up with him. I understand his crankiness a little better and am more accepting of it (well, sometimes anyway). I talk more openly with my friends and husband. I can help lots of younger folks face the trials of their lives because I've lived through them. I tell them firsthand what mistakes to avoid, as well as the fun they can have.

I'm not past my prime, I'm in it. Life is fun if you relax and enjoy it. And, at the end of every day, I'm careful to stop and thank God for my abundant blessings. I can still see, albeit with bifocals. I can still get up and go to work. I can still tease my husband and smell my dinner. I can hear the birds as they cavort in the spring—and do a little cavorting myself. I'm still a kid in God's eyes, and I intend to stay that way for the rest of my life.

Care and Counseling Tips

THE BASICS

Menopause is a natural biological process during a woman's life when the function of the ovaries ceases and periods (or menses) end. The average age for menopause is 51; however, a woman's menopause can occur at any point between her 30s and her 60s. This time in a woman's life can be dramatic or quite simple—it is different for each woman. Some physicians compare menopause to adolescence—a time of fluctuating hormones and emotions. *Periomenopause* is usually the two to five years before a woman's period stops, but sometimes women experience symptoms for 10 to 15 years before fully stopping their periods. Symptoms of menopause include:

+ Hot Flashes/Night Sweats

Women experience hot flashes differently. Some feel warm while others feel like they are burning up—their body temperature can actually rise six degrees. Sweating and reddened skin often accompany a hot flash. An episode can last anywhere from a few seconds to up to an hour, but it can take another half hour for a woman to feel like herself again. Some women feel tense and agitated during a hot flash and have heart palpitations. Hot flashes that occur during sleep are called night sweats.

+ Irregular Periods

Menstrual periods may stop suddenly or gradually get lighter or heavier and then stop. The unpredictability of a period can be unsettling for many women and may be the first clue that menopause is approaching.

+ Mood Swings/Depression

Mood swings are a common symptom for women going through menopause. Many women find themselves crying about nothing or being extremely irritable.

+ Vaginal Changes

Decreased estrogen causes the vaginal lining to thin and secretions to diminish, which can lead to vaginal dryness and irritation.

+ Weight Gain

Weight gain is a common and frustrating problem for many women in this age group.

+ Low Sexual Drive

Progesterone is crucial to libido, and the natural fall in its production during perimenopause can significantly diminish sexual desire.

+ Headaches, Dry Skin and Hair, Memory Problems, Urinary Changes, and Insomnia

These are some other symptoms some women experience during perimenopause.

Menopause is a profound time of transition for women. The combination of physical hormone changes coupled with emotions surrounding an "end of an era" can be difficult and thought provoking. Many women have an increased awareness of how finite life is, and they begin to rediscover passions and dreams for their lives that had been put on the back burner.

SCRIPTURE HELP

+ Psalm 46:1
+ Psalm 105:1-5
+ Psalm 145
+ Ecclesiastes 3:1-14
+ Isaiah 58:11

+ Matthew 6:25-34
+ Matthew 11:28-30
+ Colossians 3:15-17
+ James 5:7-8

Care Tips

+ Meet individually with the woman.
It may be very helpful to go out to coffee or have an informal one-on-one time with your friend. You can use this time to listen, encourage, and let her know you care. Help her explore whether or not her mood swings are hormonal or a result from other, nonhormone related causes such as stress (emotional and/or physical), depression, anxiety, or fatigue.

+ Get more help.
If the woman seems to be having physical or emotional issues that fall outside of the perimenopause and menopause symptoms, such as ongoing depression, refer her immediately to health care professionals.

+ Provide information.
You may want to give your friend a list of the menopause symptoms and go through it with her. This can help her realize that a lot is going on in her body during menopause and there are many physical and emotional symptoms that can come with it.

+ Recommend preventive medical help.
It's important for women to see a trusted doctor during both perimenopause and menopause. There are many different options for treating some of the symptoms as well as preventing some of the risks of menopause (such as osteoporosis), so encouraging the women in your ministry to find a good doctor is very important.

Counseling Tips

+ Validate.
It is important for the woman to feel validated in her emotional and physical journey. She needs to know she is not going crazy and she is not alone in her experiences. She also needs to know that this "change of life" does not mean life goes downhill from there!

+ Encourage the woman not to be embarrassed about what she is experiencing and to talk about it.
Often women feel uncomfortable talking about their erratic emotions and physical changes during menopause, so they keep silent. Talking to other women in the same phase of life or women who have already been through menopause can be very comforting, encouraging, and informative. Let the woman know that her emotions, questions, and concerns are common for women during this transition and are nothing to be embarrassed about.

+ Support.
Women tend to neglect their own needs and have difficulty taking time for themselves. Offer your support to the woman, and encourage her to take time to care for her needs. Taking time for adequate sleep, exercise, and diet are a few areas you can encourage her to evaluate and adjust if they are areas of neglect.

Group Tips

+ Be open and safe.

Make sure that your group provides a safe environment for women to share. Some general ways to make your group safe are: (1) letting the women know anything shared in the group will remain only in the group; (2) asking non-judgmental questions when someone shares a struggle; (3) being a warm and vulnerable group leader.

+ Lighten up together.

There are some on-the-lighter-side books about menopause that your group (or a subgroup within your group) could read together. Also, another fun activity is to go as a group to see the play *Menopause the Musical*. This comedy gives women of all ages a night filled with laughter. To see when and if the play is coming to your area, you can check out the Web site www.menopausethemusical.com.

+ Share information.

Often women can be a great resource for one another. Create an environment for your group to share things that are working or helping them with physical and emotional health and well-being. If there is a topic your women are all interested in, you might invite a guest speaker to come talk to your group on that subject.

+ Pair up.

It could be very meaningful for a perimenopausal woman to be matched up with an older woman (who has been through menopause). The relationship could be very informal, simply offering the perimenopausal woman someone she can call when she has a question or is having a rough "perimenopausal" day.

What Not to Say

✦ "Do you have those horrible headaches?"

There are plenty of problematic symptoms that accompany menopause. If the subject is raised, that's one thing, but bringing up the headaches, hot flashes, cramps, and unexpected periods just doesn't improve one's outlook.

✦ "Time to get rid of those sleeveless shirts."

When their bodies are changing, some people really don't want to hear about it. Remember your discussions about wearing a bra when you were in junior high? There were some people you wanted to talk about it with and others you really didn't.

✦ "It must be great not having your period anymore."

Women can feel less feminine and even less valuable when they go through menopause. Instead, focus on saying things that make your friend feel beautiful—inside and out.

✦ "I never experienced any of that."

When a woman shares her menopause symptoms and experiences, be sensitive when commenting on your own experiences. Though there are symptoms that many women experience during menopause, everyone's experience is different. Just listen as she shares what she is going through.

✦ "Aging is just part of life."

This sort of comment can be insensitive, particularly if a menopausal woman is grieving unfulfilled dreams and goals for her life. Instead, help your friend remember what she has accomplished in her life already, and plan for great things to come in the future.

What to Say

+ "You look terrific!"

We all like to be noticed! Point out when her hair looks good; compliment her skin. Be genuine and honest.

+ "Let's go for a walk."

Lunch is good, but a walk is better for both of you. Since this is a time when the pounds accumulate easily, look for ways to spend time doing things that don't add them.

+ "What advice do you have?"

Isn't it great to be valued? At a time when one is worrying about being forgetful and unnoticed, to be asked for advice is encouraging. She probably has some good stuff to share.

+ "Do you know what kind of menopause experience your mother had?"

This kind of question can get the woman thinking about her genetic predisposition and help her think about possible risk factors that can occur after menopause, such as heart disease and osteoporosis.

+ "How can I be praying for you?"

Sometimes women feel too embarrassed to ask for prayer for menopause-related issues. Asking to pray for the woman can let her know you validate what she is going through. You can pray with her or pray for her and follow up to see how she is doing sometime in the next week or two.

+ "Let's celebrate!"

Plan a party and celebrate life's changes rather than mourning them. Laugh and look for the positive aspects of this life change. Exchange small gifts that remind you of friends and the passages of life.

WHEN TO REFER

+ When you think the issues may fall outside of menopause

You will want to refer your woman to mental-health professionals if her behavior seems to be impacted by more than hormone changes.

+ When there are weight gain issues

Sometimes the emotional and physical effects of menopause can be further exasperated if a woman feels like her weight is out of control. If this is the case for the woman you are working with, you can refer her to a professional dietician or a dieting program sensitive to weight issues during menopause.

+ When a woman begins experiencing perimenopause symptoms

All women need to find a health care professional for her perimenopause and menopause years.

IMPORTANT FACTS

ABOUT MENOPAUSE

+ In the Western world, most women experience menopause between ages 40 and 58, the average age being 51.

+ Some women experience menopause as early as their 30s, and some as late as their 60s.

+ Smokers reach menopause about two years earlier than nonsmokers.

+ Women often experience menopause at the same age as their mothers and sisters.

ADDITIONAL RESOURCES

+ Books

What Your Doctor May Not Tell You About Premenopause: Balance Your Hormones and Your Life From Thirty to Fifty. John R. Lee, Jesse Hanley, and Virginia Hopkins. New York, NY: Grand Central Publishing, 2005.

Could It Be...Perimenopause?: How Women 35-50 Can Overcome Forgetfulness, Mood Swings, Insomnia, Weight Gain, Sexual Dysfunction, and Other Tell-Tale Signs of Hormonal Imbalance. Steven R. Goldstein and Laurie Ashner. Boston, MA: Little, Brown and Company, 2000.

Super Nutrition for Menopause: Take Control of Your Life Now and Enjoy New Vitality. Ann Louise Gittleman. Garden City Park, NY: Avery, 1998.

+ Online Resources

www.menopause.org (The North American Menopause Society)
www.mayoclinic.com/health/menopause/DS00119 (Mayo Clinic)
www.knowmenopause.com
www.menopause-online.com

CHAPTER TEN

Miscarriage
Walking With Your Friend Through the Valley of the Shadow of Death

with counseling insights from
KELLY SCHIMMEL FLANAGAN, PH.D.
+ ministry tips from LINDA CRAWFORD

I had waited a long time to become a member of the "Mom's Club." When John and I were married, we planned to wait a few years before starting a family, but not this many years. Our lives and plans for children were unexpectedly put on hold the day John received the call to active duty in the military. After being separated for two years and by too many miles, he finally returned home. We were ready to take our lives off "pause" and hit the "resume" button on starting a family.

To prepare financially for our future family, we started a business, and once that was established we were ready for that family to become a reality. The day I found out I was pregnant, I was so excited. I memorized my due date and began counting the days until our child would arrive. My dream of being a mom, of being a member of that esteemed circle of blessed women, was soon to be mine. Or so I thought…

During the sixth week of my pregnancy, I began bleeding lightly, but my midwife assured me this was normal and not to become alarmed. When it continued and became heavier by the eighth week, I visited the doctor and was scheduled for a "routine" ultrasound. Not expecting to receive bad news, my husband stayed at work and my mom went with me to the appointment. The ultrasound tech was quiet and professional throughout the exam, so I was not prepared at the end when she said, "I'm really sorry, but it doesn't look good." Devastated, I met with the midwife, and she told me they could not find a heartbeat, but they would do blood tests over the next few days to determine if the baby was really gone.

From their words, I knew there was little hope, and there was no stopping my tears from pouring out. I called my husband but couldn't speak, so my mother, through her own tears, told him, "They think Carla's losing the baby. I'm taking her home." John was equally as devastated and felt guilty about not being there. But neither of us had expected the news we received. All the hopes and dreams we had for our child and our future came crashing down.

We put a movie on "repeat" on the TV in our bedroom that night, hoping to find some distraction from our sorrow. But I sobbed and sobbed, catching only glimpses of rest. In the darkness and grief of that night, we finally lost our child.

In the days ahead, I experienced a horrible sense of loss and unfairness. We had waited so long. We had done everything right in planning for this child. Why could other women have children with no complications but not me?

After two days of tears, I tried to return to my normal routine, went back to work, small group, and women's Bible study at church. But everywhere I looked, I saw women in the Mom's Club and found myself questioning God over and over, "Why me, God? Why did this have to happen to me?"

I was exhausted physically and emotionally, yet felt I should be able to do simple things like prepare dinner. After all, I wasn't really sick or recovering from surgery, like people who usually had meals brought in. So I turned down all the generous offers from friends to bring us food. Later, I would regret doing that, as I became easily overwhelmed with the responsibility of planning and making a meal. I desperately needed rest and peace, yet in that first week of sorrow I had little of either.

I turned to my Bible to find Scriptures that would help me find that elusive peace. I circled certain passages and prayed them throughout the difficult hours of each day. I listened to worship songs that helped me focus on the goodness of God and his promise for the joy that would replace my tears. I knew if I held on to my faith, as the Lord held on to me, I would make it through the storm of grief and find a peaceful place in my broken heart.

A wonderful neighbor came to visit and cry with me during the first few painful days. I cherished her tears and those of other friends in the weeks to come. Through sharing in my sorrow, they ministered the love and acceptance I needed to begin to heal from the loss of my child.

There were many friends who offered comfort, but there were also some women in my life who withdrew and became silent after hearing of my loss. That was hard for me to understand. A close family member didn't call for weeks and later told me she "didn't know what to say," so she thought just saying nothing would be better. Though I could accept that the situation was uncomfortable for her, I felt like she had abandoned me during a time I really needed her.

But those reactions were rare. Multitudes of women in my Bible study and small group offered emotional and prayer support. Those who had experienced a miscarriage themselves were the most sensitive and empathetic to my loss and helped me feel like I was not alone in my sorrow. I needed to hear every "I'm so sorry" and receive every card and hug that came my way. I needed their prayers too, and, thankfully, my friends were not shy about praying for me in person, instead of just promising to pray and walking away. Although usually stoic and self-reliant, I know that without such a generous outpouring of love from so many women I would have mourned much longer and harder.

My husband and I had waited a long time to have a family, and we were devastated at the loss of our first child. My dreams of becoming a member of the Mom's Club had to be put on hold again, but fortunately not for long. Within months of my miscarriage, I became pregnant again. This time my excitement was tempered by anxiety. I was afraid of the possibility of enduring another devastating loss. I leaned on Scripture, prayer, and the support of my husband and friends to make it through those first critical weeks. Once again I began bleeding on the sixth week of my pregnancy. An ultrasound was scheduled, and when the technician was finished, the look on her face told John and I everything we needed to know. Our baby's beating heart was strong. We had reason to hope and dream once again.

After so many years and tears, and with the support of my family and friends, I am now an official diaper-bag toting member of the Mom's Club and I love every joyous moment!

WHEN TO REFER

+ Numbness or denial that continues and does not seem to be abating

These reactions are a normal part of the grief process, but if they are not followed by a realistic acceptance of the baby's death or appropriate emotional expression, then the woman may need to seek professional support.

+ Depression or anxiety

Severely depressed moods (such as a state of hopelessness, despair, or loneliness) are signs that a woman may need professional counseling. In addition, if intense fears about family or the future become uncontrollable and overwhelming to the woman over a two-week period or more, she may require more comprehensive mental health services. Likewise, extreme fatigue, physical complaints, and eating or sleeping disturbances can indicate depression or anxiety requiring professional help.

+ Continuance of difficulties in social functioning

Difficulty maintaining normal activities for a time after the loss is typical in the grief process, but if social withdrawal or difficulty working or taking care of the household and children continues for an extended period, professional support should be sought.

Care and Counseling Tips

THE BASICS

Miscarriage is the most common type of pregnancy loss, occurring in 10 to 25 percent of all pregnancies, though these estimates are likely low given the number of miscarriages mistaken for late menstruation. Most miscarriages occur within the first 13 weeks of a pregnancy, although miscarriage can occur at *any point* during a pregnancy. Regardless of the timing, the loss will most likely be accompanied initially by a multitude of feelings—sadness, anger, confusion, apathy, denial, disappointment, fear, and guilt. However, with the support and love of others, these feelings may eventually lead to a stronger confidence and peace in Christ's love.

There is no one reason that a miscarriage occurs, and the cause is usually not discernible. Possible causes include chromosomal abnormality, maternal hormonal or health problems, lifestyle choices (such as smoking, substance use, poor nutrition, exposure to toxic substances), improper implantation of the egg into the uterine lining, maternal trauma, and maternal age (with higher risk occurring for older women). Despite guilt-inducing myths that tend to circulate among women, miscarriage is not caused by exercise, sex, or working outside of the home. Most women are left without any medical or comprehensible explanation of why they lost the baby growing inside of them. For these mothers left without answers, a women's ministry can provide a powerful source of support. To provide support before and after a miscarriage, it is important to know its symptoms and potential results.

✛ Symptoms of a Miscarriage

Bleeding progressing from light to heavy; abdominal pain or cramping; fever, vomiting, dizziness; back pain; decrease in pregnancy signs.

✛ Potential Results of a Miscarriage

The woman's doctor will perform a pelvic exam and ultrasound to confirm the miscarriage. If the miscarriage is not complete, dilation and curettage

(D and C) or dilation and extraction (D and E) procedures will be performed in which the cervix is dilated and any remaining fetal tissue is scraped or suctioned out of the uterus. A woman may experience several days of bleeding; bed rest for several days may be prescribed then. She may experience hormonal imbalances or body image issues as the body recovers from the loss of the pregnancy, plus mood swings or depression. Blood or genetic tests, medication, or other diagnostic procedures may be used to evaluate causes of repeated miscarriages.

SCRIPTURE HELP

+ **Psalm 18:1-2**
+ **Psalm 29:11**
+ **Psalm 31:24**
+ **Psalm 34:18**
+ **Psalm 46:1**

+ **Psalm 68:19**
+ **Isaiah 41:10**
+ **Lamentations 3:21-24**
+ **Matthew 11:28-30**
+ **1 Peter 5:10**

Care Tips

As with any type of grief, it must first be recognized that each woman will experience grief *regardless* of the length of the pregnancy or the medical severity of the miscarriage, and that each will have her own grief process. One woman may not feel any sadness the day of the miscarriage but may have extreme difficulty dealing with her feelings later on. Another woman might be almost debilitated by grief the day the miscarriage occurs, but experience an abatement of that grief fairly quickly. The key is to recognize that no grieving process looks alike and that no woman should be made to feel ashamed or abnormal for having particular thoughts or feelings of grief.

✛ Treat the miscarriage as a death.

A bond between mother and baby can form quickly. Excitement, trepidation, plans for the future, or dreams or fears of having a larger family occur immediately following the "PREGNANT" indicator on the pregnancy test. The growth of another life within one's body is an amazing miracle, and the loss of this life can be heart-wrenching. For the mother-to-be, life began at conception, and she may have quickly made room for this life within her heart and her family. The resulting void may be as tangible as the death of an existing family member, and thus should not be minimized.

✛ Approach the mother in a warm, understanding manner.

Both verbal and nonverbal gestures can immediately convey your understanding of her pain. Let your words demonstrate that you take her loss seriously. Indicate that her feelings are reasonable and do not overwhelm you. Likewise, sitting silently with the mother or simply touching her arm can be a comforting gesture.

✛ Offer your support.

No one woman will have the same miscarriage experience or emotional and physical outcomes. Depending on the specifics of the miscarriage, women may have different needs. Some may need time and words of comfort and encouragement. Some may need support in daily activities due to physical complications. Some mothers may need to hear others' stories of miscarriage to normalize their own experience. If you cannot anticipate her needs, your friend will be able to tell you what she needs if you give her the chance to do so.

✛ Listen. Give the mother the chance to talk about her experience, her feelings, her loss, and her fears.

Ask the mother if she would like to talk, and then make a date to do so. You will convey your sincere desire to connect with her. Allowing time to review this experience and express her feelings and memories will facilitate the grieving process.

Counseling Tips

+ Encourage the woman to express her feelings.

As part of the grieving process, the mother must acknowledge and work through her pain rather than avoiding or suppressing it. Encourage healthy ways of expressing the pain, including journaling, creating art, praying, talking with close friends, or counseling. Initially avoiding feelings of grief, although a normal first stage of grieving for many women, may prolonged and actually hinder the mourning process.

+ Encourage feelings of normalcy.

A woman may experience many feelings after a miscarriage. She must feel comfortable experiencing and expressing these various feelings, even the difficult ones such as disappointment in and anger toward God. Do not attempt to read the woman's heart or to "know" what she is thinking and feeling. Give her room to express these feelings, evaluate them, and figure out ways to cope with them until they are more manageable.

+ Ask about guilt.

Guilt or blame is a common accompaniment to grief and may be difficult for the woman to express. The source of grief may vary—she may not have wanted the pregnancy, or she may view something she did as the cause of her baby's death. It is important to give her an opening to describe this guilt, if present. It may also be beneficial to correct any misconceptions she might have by seeking accurate medical information.

+ Encourage acceptance.

Acceptance of the loss of her baby and the close connection she may have already formed with the child will be crucial in the grieving process. Help the mother acknowledge what she feels was lost (expectations and plans, dreams for the future, or her identity as being pregnant and a mother). Also, help the woman identify new directions for the emotions she had invested in the baby; for example, focusing on the other important relationships in her life, such as a close friend, her husband, or her existing children.

✛ Encourage the involvement of family members.

The mother may not be the only one experiencing the loss of the child. Each family member will have unique ways of expressing grief. For example, her husband may be throwing himself into his work to avoid his grief, which could impact their relationship or his ability to support her. The marital relationship can provide an amazing source of strength in the grieving process, or in contrast, can increase levels of stress, guilt, sadness, or anger. Other children may have been looking forward to a new sibling—or if they weren't, they may feel guilty or responsible for the miscarriage. Help your friend identify and understand how fear, guilt, or anger is contributing to any reluctance to re-engaging in her relationships.

IMPORTANT FACTS

ABOUT MISCARRIAGE

✛ Miscarriage reportedly occurs in 20 percent of all pregnancies. However, many women may miscarry without knowing it, assuming they're experiencing heavier periods. Therefore, the miscarriage rate may be closer to 40 or 50 percent.

✛ Of the number of women who miscarry, 20 percent will suffer recurring miscarriages.

✛ Approximately 75 percent of all miscarriages occur in the first trimester.

✛ An estimated 80 percent of all miscarriages are single miscarriages. The vast majority of women suffering one miscarriage can expect to have a normal pregnancy next time.

Group Tips

✦ Lift the woman up in prayer.

It is crucial for a woman experiencing miscarriage to feel the comfort and love of those around her. Yet it is through her relationship with God that she will find the most comfort and peace. Let the mother know that she is on the group members' hearts and in their prayers. Pray for her lost child, her family, and her healing.

✦ Send notes of concern.

Individual sympathy cards or a group card can be powerful reminders to the woman of how many people she has to call upon for support, if necessary. They can represent the love that surrounds her, even though an important focus of her love has been lost. Likewise, the thought that goes into care packages, flowers, or a potted plant to place in her flower bed will be appreciated. Keep in mind what the woman might like when you are choosing such an item.

✦ Ask about the rest of her family.

Others in the mother's family may also be hurting, including her husband or children, and may not be getting the support they need. You may learn of ways you could help these family members, which in turn helps the grieving woman.

✦ Be ready to listen.

At all times, be ready to listen to the mother. You may not know, nor may she, when she will need to talk through her feelings, thoughts, or memories. She may need to tell the story of her miscarriage again and again, and your openness to allowing this expression will help her in her grief process.

+ You may not know what to say or do, but do not remain silent.

If the grieving woman is closely connected to your ministry, she needs the group's support. Recognize that your words can either harm or help, so think carefully about what you want to say before the words are out. Each group member should recognize her own possible discomfort with death, and let it inform her interactions with the woman. Some group members may feel more comfortable organizing a cleaning group to go to the woman's house, others may feel gifted in listening and empathizing due to their own experience with miscarriage, and still others may do a wonderful job preparing meals or a care package.

+ Offer the group's help.

Make yourselves available to help the mother in any way she might need, particularly as she may be physically and emotionally strained. She may need nutritious food for herself and her family. She may need help with household chores or child care. She may need time to be alone or to be with her husband without worrying about her children.

+ Help the woman decide if and how she wants to remember her lost child.

Every woman will have different desires with regard to remembrances of her baby. Some women may want to name the child, hold a small memorial service, or plant a flowering bush or a tree for the child. Some women may want to reconnect with their husbands and have time to grieve with them. The group can help the woman identify her desires and make plans to achieve them.

What Not to Say

✚ "Don't worry, God will give you another baby."

This is similar to statements like "Well, at least you have little Mikey," that not-so-subtly invalidate your friend's grief and imply other children can replace the loss of her child. Let your friend know it's OK to experience sorrow. Offer a supportive shoulder to help her navigate through the emotions and emptiness she feels. Validate her tears—don't try to take them away.

✚ "God would not permit pain in your life that you could not handle."

The problem of pain has always been a difficult one to address, and doing so in the midst of the mother's grief is not the appropriate time. Rather, help her know that God can sustain her through the pain and provide comfort, rather than implying that God caused, or at the very least, did not act to prevent her loss.

✚ "It is for the best. The baby was probably deformed."

The mother will not benefit from being told that her miscarriage was better than the child living to full-term. It is OK for the woman to come to this conclusion on her own, but death should never be referred to as the best option. Recognize how quickly the mother may have become attached to the life growing inside of her, and consider how much a statement like this might hurt.

✚ "It's better that it happened so early."

This statement will likely invoke instant tears in a woman who has experienced a recent miscarriage. From the moment she found out she was pregnant, she counted the days and believed for the future of her child. To her, you have just invalidated the reality of the profound loss of that life and her future dreams. Remember that whether it's weeks in the womb or years on the planet, all life is precious.

What to Say

✛ "I'm so sorry for your loss."

A simple "I'm sorry" is sufficient, particularly if you cannot find the words to speak with the woman. Accompany your words with a hug or just hold her hand. These most likely will be taken as unexpected, simple gestures of understanding and caring that will be greatly appreciated.

✛ "It's OK to cry; your baby is worth crying about."

Offer permission to the mother to grieve openly, as the ability to express her feelings will influence how her mourning will progress and be resolved.

✛ "God cares for you. He understands your pain, your confusion, your anger, and can handle them all."

Our God is a God who has suffered and understands all the pain that this woman feels. Convey to her that all her feelings are normal and not too big for him to bear. Remind her that God cares for her and understands the suffering she is experiencing and wants to comfort her.

✛ "Please know that I am here to listen for as long as you need."

Follow up with your friend, even past what you might think of as a "normal" time to grieve. Mourning can last anywhere between a few months to a few years. Further, a following pregnancy may elicit feelings of grief or fear. Check in with your friend regularly, which will demonstrate your concern, your support, and your openness to listen both now and in the future.

✛ "I'm here for you; can I pray for you?"

Many women say "I'll pray for you" and walk away. Instead, let the person know you are active in your promises and offer to pray for them on the spot or at a future date. You don't want to be pushy, but convey with your actions that you are not making an empty promise. She needs you and she needs your prayers. Be a visible support, not an invisible promise.

ADDITIONAL RESOURCES

+ Books

I'll Hold You in Heaven: Healing and Hope for the Parent Who Has Lost a Child Through Miscarriage, Stillbirth, Abortion or Early Infant Death. Jack Hayford. Ventura, CA: Regal Books, 2003.

Empty Arms: Hope and Support for Those Who Have Suffered a Miscarriage, Stillbirth or Tubal Pregnancy. Pam Vredevelt. Colorado Springs, CO: Multnomah Publishers, Inc. 2001.

An Empty Cradle, a Full Heart: Reflections for Mothers and Fathers After Miscarriage, Stillbirth, or Infant Death. Christine O'Keefe Lafser. Chicago, IL: Loyola Press, 1998.

In Heavenly Arms: Grieving the Loss and Healing the Wounds of Miscarriage. Shari Bridgeman. Lake Forest, CA: BlackHawk Canyon Publishers, 1997.

+ Online Resources

www.nationalshareoffice.com (Share: Pregnancy and Infant Loss Support, Inc.)

www.mend.org (Mommies Enduring Neonatal Death)

www.aplacetoremember.com

www.troubledwith.com/LoveandSex/Miscarriage.cfm (a Web site of Focus on the Family)

CHAPTER ELEVEN

Rape
Supporting Women After a Sexual Assault

with counseling insights from **TERRI S. WATSON, PSY.D.**
+ ministry tips from **LINDA CRAWFORD**

Anna despises NASCAR racing. Her stomach turns every time she sees a commercial for a NASCAR event on TV. But her aversion has nothing to do with the sport itself and everything to do with an image of a NASCAR poster seared onto her mind. It was the only thing she found she could focus on in a darkened room nearly 10 years ago—a room where she endured being sexually assaulted by a young man she barely knew. She had clearly said "no," but found herself utterly powerless to stop him from raping her.

Although able to share freely about her experience now, at the time Anna was too traumatized to tell anyone. She was a young college student, who, like many of her peers, had drifted away from her Christian faith as she was drawn by friends into the college party scene. Her social life revolved around drinking and partying with friends. On the night of the assault, Anna was at a party when she accepted a ride home from two young men...only they never took her home. Feeling vulnerable and trapped, Anna was unable to resist or deter the unwanted advances that followed when they drove her to their apartment. She endured the harrowing dark hours of the night staring at the NASCAR poster and anxiously awaited the light of sunrise to help her plan an escape from the nightmare.

When the men finally dropped her off at her friend's house the following morning, Anna, though severely traumatized, decided to keep silent about what had happened.

"I did not report anything, and I did not tell anyone. I was blaming myself for being in the situation, especially because of the drinking involved. I didn't deserve to be treated like that, but I felt that I basically put myself there."

Unable to process the unbearable emotional pain she felt from being raped, in the months that followed, Anna tried to bury it instead. She turned to alcohol to help numb her feelings of anger, guilt, and shame. Believing she had lost her value as a woman from the sexual assault, Anna sank into depression and a cycle of destructive behaviors including smoking and promiscuity. After six months, her drinking and partying had become so out of hand she was forced to drop out of school for a semester. But still she kept the truth of her anguish hidden and stifled any thoughts of seeking help. When she finally did confide her tormenting secret to a few friends, they only supported her in placing the blame on herself and encouraged her to avoid pressing charges.

"Somebody said, 'Well I'm proud of you for not turning him in because you were drinking.' The implication was that I was part of the problem."

As time went on, Anna felt more helpless to do anything about what had happened to her. She concluded that seeking prosecution wouldn't change what had already happened and feared that it would only make things worse. So she continued to suffer alone, separated from God and from people who could give her the love she so desperately needed.

During the difficult, silent years that followed, Anna repeatedly and despairingly wrote in her journal, *"I have a hole in my heart."* But it wasn't until the topic of rape was brought up in a college class three years after her assault that Anna's real feelings were jolted to the surface. As the discussion of rape continued in the class, Anna began to feel the emotions she had labored to restrain suddenly erupt to the surface. Unable to control the intensity of her suffering any longer, she bolted from the lecture hall sobbing uncontrollably.

It was an excruciatingly painful turning point that led Anna to seek counseling and begin a gradual journey out of her depression and destructive lifestyle, and back to God. As she processed her emotional pain from the rape, she wrote a poem entitled *I Hate NASCAR*. But Anna found that venting her feelings at NASCAR wasn't enough, she had to dig deeper to discover what would begin to fill that long-standing hole in her heart.

"I didn't believe I was loved by people, or by God. I wanted the love and I wanted the acceptance, but I was going about it completely the wrong way. I knew I was trying to fill the hole, and I also knew that God was the only one who could fill it."

But even though Anna knew she had to find her way back to God, she had trouble getting back to church and connecting with other believers in her hometown. Finally, after many failed attempts to change her life, she decided to leave the surroundings of her past behind and move to another state to start over. Once there, she secured a job and began attending church again. She joined a ministry group where women shared their stories of sexual abuse and supported and loved each other through their healing process. Anna also began work to recapture the beauty and value of her body by adopting a healthy lifestyle and indulging herself in some pampering. While the manicures and pedicures didn't miraculously heal her emotional pain, they did help her regain her sense of value and self-worth.

The unconditional love and willingness to listen she received from her support group helped Anna become more open about sharing her story. Within the church she received mixed reactions to her confession of the events of her previous life. One woman thanked her and said, "I didn't know there were other people in the church like me." But there were also those who reacted with shock when they found out that Anna actually worked for the church, asking, "Does the church know about all this?"

Despite those few negative responses, Anna remained committed to sharing her story, to help other hurting women realize there was hope for healing after rape. It took years of struggling and searching, but she was finally able to talk about how finding her way back to God had changed her life.

"I made some bad choices—all because I wanted love. But without the struggles I had, I would probably not be the Christian I am today. I would probably just be a 'go to church on Sunday' person and not really have a connection to God or other people."

Almost 10 years after she was raped, Anna still struggles whenever "NASCAR" flashes on a TV screen. The images, the pain, and the shame of that terrible night still flood back, but Anna's healthy now and discovering the love that will fill that hole in her heart—God's love and unconditional love from others. But she admits that *"it takes a powerful love"* to penetrate the pain and minister to a rape victim's heart.

"Saying 'I love you' once won't change anything. Saying 'I love you even though I don't understand you,' and 'I love you even when you walked out on dinner when NASCAR came on TV'...That's the kind of unconditional love that makes a difference."

IMPORTANT FACTS

ABOUT RAPE

✚ One out of every six women in the U.S. has been a victim of sexual assault.

✚ Nine out of every 10 rape victims is female.

✚ About 44 percent of victims are under the age of 18.

✚ An estimated 59 percent of rapes are unreported by victims.

✚ Two-thirds of rapes are committed by someone who is known to the victim.

Care and Counseling Tips

THE BASICS

Few crimes against women are more traumatic than the experience of sexual assault. Sexual assault is defined as unwanted sexual contact, including touching and fondling. Rape is the most severe form of sexual assault and involves forced sexual intercourse or penetration of any part of the body with a body part or object. Most sexual assaults are committed by someone known to the victim. Most of these crimes go unreported because of the shame, embarrassment, and self blame that victims often experience. Many women have never revealed their experience of sexual trauma to anyone. It is highly likely that some of these "silent victims" are in your women's ministry right now. Understanding the physical, emotional, and spiritual effects of sexual assault is an important first step in providing a caring, Christian response.

+ Initial Effects

The terror, sense of violation, and fear of loss of life that most victims experience produce a combination of post-traumatic stress symptoms. Survivors may initially exhibit shock, disbelief, and fear. They are likely to think about the trauma constantly and have flashbacks, nightmares, difficulty sleeping, headaches, and loss of appetite. Some victims may be very tearful and angry, while others will appear calm and controlled. Feelings of guilt, self-blame, and shame are likely to be a part of a survivor's initial reaction. They may feel overwhelmed with the practical demands facing them, which may include seeking medical attention, giving a report to the police, and telling loved ones about the crime.

+ Ongoing Effects

After several weeks, women begin to re-engage in their normal life activities, and may seek to put the trauma behind them. They may attempt to deny or avoid thinking about what has happened, but are likely to continue to experience anxiety, anger, depressive symptoms, shame, and feelings of vulnerability. They may become socially isolated as their feelings of shame and self-blame cause them to pull away from others close to them. Women who do not tell anyone about their assault are particularly at risk for depression, suicidal thoughts, substance abuse, and self-destructive behaviors. Rape victims who experienced the trauma years ago, but are just now telling others about it, may re-experience the trauma as if it had just occurred.

+ Spiritual Effects

Sexual assault victims often feel spiritually confused and distant from God. They may believe that the assault was punishment by God for their thoughts or behaviors, or was a 'test' of their character. Many victims experience a crisis of trust in their relationship with God and feel disillusioned that he failed to protect them from harm. Christian victims of sexual assault may feel that they are too "dirty" or "tainted" to seek comfort from God and from others in the church. They may not tell others in the church about the rape, for fear that they will judge or blame them for the sexual assault. Victims need the church to be a safe, nonjudgmental, healing place where they can work through the difficult spiritual impact of the trauma.

Care Tips

Bringing the love of Christ to sexual assault victims in tangible ways is a key component of the healing process, and can begin to restore the victim's trust and hope in God and others. The nonjudgmental, loving support of a Christian community can help the sexual assault victim work through the traumatic aftereffects and provide them with spiritual and relational resources for healing. How can the small group help? The following suggestions address specific ways to respond when someone in your small group discloses their experience of a sexual assault.

✛ Listen, believe, and accept.

Assault survivors may need to tell their story multiple times as they begin to work through the traumatic experience and struggle with difficult questions about the meaning and impact of the assault on their lives. Telling the story of the sexual trauma is the first step toward healing. Listen with patience and without judgment. Believe her. Women rarely "make up" sexual assault experiences. Don't press for details—allow her to decide how much she tells you about what happened. Affirm her for taking the courageous step to tell others about the rape. Remember that it *is* rape—even if it happened on a date, even if she didn't fight or say no, or even if she was passed out, asleep, or doesn't remember. Protect her privacy by not sharing her experiences with others without her permission.

✛ Tell her it is not her fault.

Survivors blame themselves for their trauma. Assure her that, no matter what she did or didn't do, the sexual assault was not her fault. Then, assure her again! Be careful not to subtly convey blame by asking her what she was wearing, if she fought her attacker, whether she said "no," or if she had too much to drink. It is extremely important that caregivers refrain from the human tendency to "blame the victim" by sending clear and consistent messages to the victim that she is not at fault for her victimization.

Remind her that the blame lies entirely with her attacker, who chose to commit the crime.

+ Encourage action.

Offer to help her take the necessary steps to ensure her safety, health, and recovery. If the rape has just occurred, it is imperative that her safety is the first priority. Offer to call the police, to take her to the hospital emergency room, and to stay with her during the medical exam and police interview. Tell her not to clean up, shower, change clothes, or brush her teeth, so that the necessary legal evidence can be gathered. Encourage her to call the National Sexual Assault Hotline (1-800-656-HOPE) and ask a trained advocate to walk her through the legal and medical procedures and explain her choices. Support her right to decide whether she prosecutes her abuser, whether you agree with her or not.

When someone discloses a sexual assault that has happened in the past, action steps are still important and can restore a sense of empowerment and competence to the victim. Encourage her to talk with a rape crisis counselor and explore her options. If she has not had a medical exam since the assault, encourage her to do so, and talk with her physician about any concerns. Offer to go with her to the police to explore legal options. If she is willing, help her tell significant others in her life (spouse, parents, siblings) about her rape.

+ Provide spiritual care.

Assure her that it is not God's will for her to experience sexual trauma, nor is it a punishment for anything she has done or not done. Commit to her that you will "bear this burden" with her and be a faithful companion to her on her journey toward healing and recovery. Pray with her for justice, healing, and restoration. Help her utilize important spiritual resources, such as reading and meditating on Scripture, journaling her conversations with God, worshipping God through listening to and singing praise music, and giving to others through service. Eventually, as she has progressed through the healing process, you can help her with the difficult task of forgiving her attacker and reclaiming a life of joy and hope.

Counseling Tips

Helping her heal from sexual assault will require spiritual maturity, consistent care, and patience on your part. Although every experience is different, a majority of sexual assault victims require at least a year to recover from their ordeal and reclaim their lives. Supportive relationships can make all the difference during this time.

+ Foster her resilience.

Explore with her how she has survived difficult times of suffering in the past, and encourage her to capitalize on her "natural resources." Healthy coping skills can include: maintaining an optimistic outlook, reminding oneself of God's faithfulness in the past, seeking out supportive relationships, utilizing humor, and finding meaning and purpose in the midst of suffering. Spiritual resources such as prayer, meditating on Scripture, and worship will likely be key for her as well, as she seeks the strength to recover from her traumatic experience.

+ Gently address her false beliefs about herself, her relationships, God, and the future.

Traumatic experiences such as sexual assault can have a dramatic impact on the victim's perspective because she can begin to view herself and the world through the lens of the assault. Empathize with the despair and anger she may feel, but gently provide a "corrective" view with the truths of Scripture. For example, a negative statement about herself, such as "I'm damaged beyond repair," can be responded to by saying "I understand that you feel like you've been broken by this experience, but I trust God for your healing and restoration, even if you can't trust him right now."

+ Help her find a support group for sexual trauma victims.

It can be invaluable for rape victims to talk with others who have had similar experiences. Most communities have a rape crisis center that provides a support group for trauma victims. You can look in your local phone book or call the hotline number mentioned on page 148 to find support groups in your area. Online support groups are available if she does not feel ready to talk to anyone in person.

+ Get the support that you need.

Providing care for a victim of sexual assault can stir up many feelings for caregivers, including anxiety, anger, and helplessness. It is imperative that you and others in your small group have trusted people to talk with (other than the victim) about your own feelings and reactions. This is especially important if you have experienced trauma in your own life. Taking care of yourself and getting the support you need will help you be able to care for your friend throughout her recovery.

SCRIPTURE HELP

+ Psalm 13
+ Psalm 31:24
+ Psalm 46:1
+ Psalm 68:19
+ Proverbs 3:5-6

+ Isaiah 41:10
+ Isaiah 43:2-3
+ Habakkuk 3:16-19
+ Ephesians 3:14-21
+ 2 Thessalonians 2:16-17

Group Tips

+ Help her feel safe.

For many sexual assault victims, dealing with the day-to-day feelings of anxiety, vulnerability, panic, and fear can be the most difficult part of recovery. Ask her regularly what she needs from you to help manage these feelings. Be available to pray with her; talk with her on the phone; and accompany her to doctor's visits, court proceedings, and the police station. Offer to stay with her overnight, or let her stay with you if she feels particularly anxious at nighttime.

+ Help with the practical matters.

This is a critical time for your group to step up and help her with all of the details of her life that may fall by the wayside while she attempts to cope with the trauma. Providing child care, meals, grocery shopping, and cleaning her house are all tangible ways to demonstrate support and care to her. Help her maintain a sense of control over her life by encouraging her to make the necessary decisions, while your group plays a "supporting" role.

+ Put together a "toolbox" for coping with anxiety.

Make a small notebook for her with passages of Scripture, inspirational quotes, and words of encouragement that she can carry around with her. Give her CDs of her favorite, soothing Christian music to listen to in the car. Gifts of items that will help her soothe herself and care for herself, like candles or bubble bath, may also be helpful.

+ Help her reclaim her life.

Provide her with a list of activities she can do with group members that help her reconnect with others, with God, and with her life. Put together a "coupon book" for her with specific outings to do with group members, such as "Call Joan for a walk on the beach" or "movie night with Lisa" or "praise and worship service with Deborah." Don't be afraid to initiate outings with her; she may need a little prompting to re-engage with others.

+ Physical touch?

It is important to take your cues from her when it comes to demonstrations of physical affection. If you are not sure, ask her if you could give her a hug or hold onto her hand during a difficult time.

ADDITIONAL RESOURCES

+ Books

Sexual Assault: Will I Ever Feel Okay Again? Kay Scott. Minneapolis, MN: Bethany House Publishers, 1993.

Invisible Wounds. Candace Walters. Portland, OR: Multnomah Press, 1987.

+ Online Resources

www.rainn.org (Rape, Abuse, and Incest National Network)
www.ibiblio.org/rcip (Rape Crisis Information; online support groups)

What Not to Say

+ "Are you sure that's what happened?"

Rape victims are very fearful that others won't believe them. Make sure she understands that you accept her story as true. Once they have told others about the sexual assault, they will also be concerned that others may view them as sinful, dirty, or tarnished. Make a special effort to seek her out, sit with her at church, and stay connected with her through phone calls and e-mails.

+ "Try to put it out of your mind and think about something else."

Avoiding, denying, or minimizing the assault can actually impede her recovery. It is in the remembering and retelling that healing and growth can occur.

+ "God is trying to tell you something."

Do not encourage the victim to see the sexual assault as God's punishment, plan, or intervention. Not only is this hurtful to the victim, it is not biblical. Rape is never God's intention for his beloved children. The innocent throughout history have suffered from the sinful, evil acts and choices of others. Help her trust in God's providence, believe in her innocence, and see clearly that the act was the result of the sinful choices of the attacker.

+ "Well, you'd been drinking—what did you expect?"

Don't judge her, or her actions, at the time of the assault. Often, well-meaning friends and family can add to the victim's self-blame by asking "why" questions ("Why were you walking alone at night in the city?"). This only puts the blame on the victim, rather than the rapist, who committed the crime. Remember, for most victims, their only thought is survival. Affirm her for successfully surviving the attack.

What to Say

+ "How can we help you feel safe?"

It may be difficult for her to ask for what she needs to feel safe and calm. Ask her on a regular basis what would be helpful to her. Take your cues from her.

+ "It is not your fault this happened."

You may feel like a "broken record," but your friend may need to hear this message many times, in as many different ways as you can think of. Help her keep her focus on her successful survival and the strength she has demonstrated since that time.

+ "It's OK to be angry."

Many Christian women do not know what to do with angry thoughts and feelings. Intense feelings of anger, rage, and injustice are normal reactions to sexual assault. Victims may feel angry toward their attacker, God, and significant others. Encourage her to find healthy, safe outlets for expression; including journaling, exercise, and venting to a trusted friend or professional counselor. For many women, pursuing justice through prosecution of their attacker becomes an important channel for their sense of anger and injustice.

WHEN TO REFER

✚ Child abuse

If the sexual assault occurred when your friend was under 18, or if you learn of a child who was recently assaulted, you must report the incident to Child Protective Services. The National Child Abuse Hotline number is 1-800-4-A-CHILD.

✚ Provide her with contact information for rape crisis hotlines, Web sites, and crisis centers in your community

Victims of sexual assault are able to negotiate the many legal, medical, and emotional challenges more successfully with the help of an experienced rape crisis counselor. Advocates in your community can provide a wealth of knowledge and experience that can provide the rape victim with much-needed resources and information.

✚ Medical care

Even if she thinks she is physically OK, a sexual assault victim should always seek medical attention. Medical examination and testing can rule out injury or sexually transmitted diseases, and can provide important legal evidence in the event that the victim decides to prosecute.

✚ Professional counseling

Professional help from a counselor experienced with sexual assault victims can speed the healing process. If your group member exhibits suicidal thoughts, self-destructive behaviors, increased isolation, or problems functioning at school or work, it is imperative that she receive professional help. Counseling services can often be funded through the Crime Victims Assistance Fund, which can be accessed through your local police department.

CHAPTER TWELVE

Sexual Orientation
Equipping Women to Make Wise Sexual Choices

with counseling insights from **RENEE MADISON, LPC**
+ ministry tips from **CHRISTINA SCHOFIELD**

Meghan was lonely in her marriage, and her friendships weren't satisfying. She found herself craving companionship and intimacy with another woman. "I was looking for my lost mom, although I couldn't articulate that to anyone for a long time," she tells. "I was a little girl in an adult body...I wanted desperately to be accepted, yearning for a woman to make me feel special, comfort me, hold me, value me, spend time with me, tell me who I am, look into my soul." Meghan met a kindred spirit, a young mom at the park. They had a lot in common, and it seemed to Meghan that she had found the kind of friendship she'd been longing for. But the admiration she felt turned into dependency and attraction.

"Out of desperation from the inner turmoil I was experiencing, I eventually confessed my struggle and began the healing journey," Meghan shares. She began counseling and an intense program designed to bring healing to those who are sexually and relationally broken. "I invited a small community of family and friends to walk with me—people who love Jesus and believe in his forgiveness and power to transform lives." They have been her comrades in battle, praying and encouraging her with Scripture.

Meghan's faith and walk with Christ are notable; her knowledge of the

Bible is amazing. She agreed to an interview in an effort to reach out to others struggling with this kind of turmoil and temptation, to let them know they are not alone in their battle for purity.

Emergency Response Handbook: *What should a person dealing with this struggle do to protect her heart from temptation?*

Meghan: Avoid building an exclusive relationship with another woman where all other relationships are neglected. Cultivate a variety of friendships. Avoid isolation. Avoid sharing your feelings with the person you are struggling with. Confess to safe, healthy, Christ-like others. Ask God for wisdom. Avoid situations where you will be vulnerable to temptation.

ERH: *What can help a person cope with this struggle?*

Meghan: I've found it's important to be honest with myself and others. I always stop to ask, "What are my true motivations?" I spend regular time reading and meditating on God's Word. Jesus is the one who truly does satisfy me, and his Word transforms my mind (Romans 12:1-2).

I've also found community to be important, through small groups or a healing program. Conferences can help, as can seeing a counselor on a regular basis. I've developed accountability relationships where there is transparency, and the truth is spoken in love. There are lots of ways to avoid isolation.

ERH: *How have others helped you in your struggle?*

Meghan: A growing group of family and friends have made a commitment to stand with me for the long haul on this healing journey to wholeness. Their resolve has been demonstrated by their actions and consistent prayer, over time. When I'm too tired to fight, they come alongside me and hold my arms up until there is victory (Exodus 17:10-13). These people help me see God moving in my life, the positive changes that are occurring in me.

ERH: *What things have people said or done that have been hurtful?*

Meghan: Asking, "When are you going to be healed?" "How long is this going to take?" Telling me that the solution is to just focus on my marriage—read books on kindling romance in my marriage. In ignorance, people comment on how they just can't understand how women can actually "like" each other like that, and then shudder with disdain.

ERH: *What feelings have you had to work through during this struggle?*

Meghan: I've felt ashamed, lonely, and angry. There are feelings of grief, pain, longing, need, and confusion. These feelings can lead to real depression and the fear of intimacy.

ERH: *Describe the kind of relationship you think God wants for you.*

Meghan: I think idolatry is at the center of a same-sex attraction struggle. It's worshipping and seeking one's identity in a woman instead of God. God wants our relationships to be free of control—mutual, open handed, able to give and receive and at their core, honoring. God is the one you seek to satisfy your longings and desires.

Press into your relationship with Jesus, getting to know him more fully. Lay down the masks and facades, and ask God to help you discover your true self.

Meghan concludes with a challenge, "Don't settle for breadcrumbs when God is offering you a feast. I mistook the breadcrumbs of broken relationships for a feast, but ultimately they always left me unsatisfied, wanting more. As I've ventured further down the road on this healing journey, God has reminded me that I've been invited to eat at his table. I don't have to settle for breadcrumbs.

Care and Counseling Tips

THE BASICS

The media bombards women with inappropriate and unrealistic images of "ideal" appearance and sexual behavior. It's easy to become confused about what women should be thinking or feeling, and they may compare themselves with role models they see in magazines or on TV. This confusion can lead to issues with gender identity and same-sex attraction. Though these two topics are not the same thing, some women may experience both.

As a ministry leader, you're likely to come across women who are struggling with their identity, or may even be attracted to other women sexually. They may feel fear or shame and may not be comfortable sharing their experiences unless they know that you will react with Christian love and journey with them nonjudgmentally.

✛ Understand the terms.

Sex: biological male/femaleness.

Gender: psychological or behavioral characteristics associated with biological males and females.

Gender Identity: basic discrimination of males from females and a sense of belonging to one sex.

Gender Role: behaviors, attitudes, and personality traits that a given cultural/historical society designate as more appropriate to masculine/feminine.

Sexual Orientation: gender and age of the persons to whom one is attracted sexually.

Sexual Identity: who/how one regards oneself to be as a sexual being.

Same-Sex Attraction: the sexual attraction to a member of the same gender.

✛ Understand subtle signs.

Women experiencing these types of struggles may manifest their inner conflict in a variety of ways. Common examples may include withdrawal from women or a desire to have one "best friend" or "special friend" whom they feel they can control in a relationship. They may dress in masculine clothes, hiding the feminine features that God gave them. They may compare themselves to other women and feel inferior.

SCRIPTURE HELP

+ **Psalm 19:7-14**
+ **Psalm 139**
+ **Psalm 147:3**

+ **Romans 12:9-10**
+ **Hebrews 4:14-16**
+ **Hebrews 12:1-13**
+ **1 Peter 1:22**

MINISTRY TIP

The *Girlfriends Unlimited* ministry has a great example of why it's so important to welcome all women into your ministry. *Girlfriends Unlimited* received an e-mail from a woman looking for a homosexual relationship. She had mistaken the ministry's name for a dating site.

Instead of rejecting her, they invited her to one of their meetings. When she showed up, they welcomed her with acceptance and love. She kept attending and they kept accepting her. As a result, this young woman came to believe in Jesus, which changed her thinking and behavior.

Care Tips

If a woman in your ministry expresses conflict about her sexual identity, your first reaction should be one of Christian love and compassion. Even admitting such a conflict probably cost the woman a great deal of inner turmoil and fear. Judgment or rejection now might prevent her from ever discussing the subject again, and might drive her deeper into her own private despair.

Meet her where she is. Let her know that you care about her and want to listen and help. The following tips may be of assistance:

✛ Stay calm.
Don't be alarmed by these disclosures. If you seem surprised or embarrassed, you might send the message that it's not OK to talk about tough subjects in your ministry. Take a deep breath and remember that God is bigger than our problems—he can and *does* heal where we feel less than whole.

✛ Take the issue seriously.
Our gender and sexuality is core to who we are. When women don't feel loved for who they are, they will begin to reject themselves.

✛ Involve and love everyone.
We are broken in relationship—and we are healed in relationship. Women dealing with core issues of gender and sexuality need to be accepted for who they are now, and need to know that there are those who are willing to walk with them as them as they struggle to become the women God intended.

✛ Don't make one sexual sin worse than another.
Some groups will embrace women who are pregnant outside of marriage with grace and mercy, but when a woman begins questioning her sexual

orientation, they turn away coldly. Embrace all people in your ministry, reject all sin equally, and love all sinners equally.

+ Continue the conversation.
Remember that sexual development is a journey that happens over a lifetime, not a single event that happens in adolescence or young adulthood. Keep the door open for continued nonjudgmental discussion about the topics of homosexuality and gender identity.

WHEN TO REFER

Those who struggle with same-sex attraction may need an ex-gay ministry and/or professional counselor. Gender identity issues may need some professional counseling to work out past wounding from others and rejection of self.

IMPORTANT FACTS

ABOUT SEXUAL ORIENTATION
+ There are not reliable statistics on homosexuality, but some researchers project that approximately 5 percent of the population is homosexual.
+ Homosexuality was classified as a mental disorder until 1973.
+ In a study done in the mid-1990s, about one-fifth of lesbians in the study were the victims of hate crimes.
+ There are laws against discrimination on the basis of sexual orientation in 10 U.S. states.

Counseling Tips

+ Understand homosexuality.

Homosexuality may be the result of the interaction of environmental influences, relational deficits, and inherent individual characteristics and temperaments. No gene has been found that indicates women or men are born homosexual. Instead, it is a complex and often a profound pattern of thinking and behavior that may have begun early in life. When a woman doesn't receive what she needs in order to be affirmed and loved as a woman, she may reject men and desire the love and attention of other women. Those needs may become sexualized.

+ Openly communicate about what she needs.

Have a serious conversation with your friend about her needs. She may need to open up to other women in a safe environment to counter the fear of being rejected and unloved. She may need help with ending an unhealthy relationship. She may want someone to teach her what it's like to be a healthy woman—in dress, mannerism, relationships, and so on.

+ Follow up.

There is great debate about the ability to change homosexual attraction and behavior. It is possible for men and women to develop healthier relational patterns, purity in their sexuality, and solidity in their sense of self and gender identity. As with any life change, you can help your friend by continuing to stand by her as she enters into deeper intimacy with God.

+ Fight isolation.

Walking in wholeness and integrity is possible. Temptation to rely on unhealthy relationships to meet relational and identity needs do not have to control or rule your friend's life. This strength and wholeness takes time. Help the women in your ministry set healthy boundaries in relationships, both old and new, with men and women. Consider creating a support group, or help your friend establish a healthy mentor relationship with a strong Christian woman or couple in your church.

ADDITIONAL RESOURCES

+ Books

A Broken Image: Restoring Personal Wholeness Through Healing Prayer. Leanne Payne. Grand Rapids, MI: Baker, 1995.

Emotional Dependency. Lori Rentzel. Downers Grove, IL: InterVarsity Press, 1990.

The Heart of Female Sex Attraction: A Comprehensive Counseling Resource. Janelle Hallman. Downers Grove, IL: InterVarsity Press, 2008.

Restoring Sexual Identity: Hope for Women Who Struggle with Same-Sex Attraction. Anne Paulk. Eugene, OR: Harvest House Publishers, 2003.

+ Online Resources

http://www.exodus.to (Exodus International)
http://www.desertstream.org (Desert Stream Ministries)

Group Tips

+ Create a welcoming atmosphere in your ministry.

Welcome all women into your ministry. Show Jesus' love to all women in your ministry. Demonstrate the compassion and acceptance Jesus shows to each of us. Model the kindness and patience that God shows to each of us. Make Romans 2:4 a cornerstone of your ministry: "Don't you see how wonderfully kind, tolerant, and patient God is with you? Does this mean nothing to you? Can't you see that his kindness is intended to turn you from your sin?"

+ Establish an attitude of accountability.

Every member of the group needs to be accountable to one another. The group needs to be a safe place to be known—not rejected—to allow personal growth.

+ Examine attributes of Christ-like women.

We are all on a journey of making relational and sexual choices that are pleasing to God. Challenge all of the women in your ministry to read and apply Proverbs 31 to their lives. Consider a group study about what femininity means, both to society and to God.

+ Pray together.

Prayer reminds us that God is bigger than our struggles. Model reliance on God through prayer. Your example will help the women in your ministry connect with God, where all true strength and change come from. Group prayer is an important and supportive way of connecting with others and with God.

What Not to Say

+ "I just can't relate."
At the heart of Jesus' ministry was his ability to meet people where they were and love them. Jesus, though perfect, was drawn toward and related to those trapped in the most desperate and vicious sins because he loved intensely. Let genuine love and concern compel you to get past your reservations and help in any way you can.

+ "God hates homosexuality."
The Bible uses strong language when it warns against all sexual sins, but the toughest words were saved for the Pharisees—those duplicitous folk who ranked sins and were sure they were better than everyone else. Speak with compassion and love. None of us is fit to judge.

+ "Just start dating men."
Insecurity will not be healed by dating or having a relationship with a man. The need for women is to be comfortable "in their own skin" as women.

+ "This is the worst sin."
Jesus died for all sins equally. All sins separate us from God.

What to Say

+ "God is a healer."
Perhaps even more amazing than God's grace and forgiveness is his ability to completely restore and transform us. Remind your friend that we are each a work in progress. If anyone is in Christ, she is a new creation!

+ "I will always be your friend."
Aren't you glad God gives us second, third, and fourth chances? Don't let a

friend lose this battle because she is consumed by guilt and shame. Be there for the victories and the setbacks, encouraging with prayer and Scripture.

+ "God gives strength."

Battling temptation is exhausting and impossible in our own strength. But the Bible says that through God's Holy Spirit, we can overcome sin and temptation. That's a promise. Pass it on!